Bug Bounty Success

How to Become a Top Earner in the Bug Bounty Community

James Moore

Welcome to **"Bug Bounty Success: How to Become a Top Earner in the Bug Bounty Community"**! I'm *James Moore*, and I'm excited to share my knowledge and experiences in the world of bug bounties with you.

For as long as I can remember, I've been fascinated by the intricacies of cybersecurity and the ever-evolving threats that surround our digital landscape. My journey into bug bounties began as a hobby, an exploratory venture into the world of ethical hacking. Little did I know that this passion would lead me to become a top earner in the bug bounty community.

Bug bounty programs have gained significant momentum in recent years, becoming crucial components of organizations' security strategies. These programs provide a unique opportunity for security researchers like us to uncover vulnerabilities in companies' digital infrastructure, helping them improve their security posture while earning substantial rewards.

In this book, I aim to guide you through the intricate process of becoming a successful bug bounty hunter. Whether you're just starting out or already have some experience under your belt, this comprehensive guide will equip you with the knowledge, strategies, and mindset required to excel in this exciting field.

We'll begin by laying a strong foundation, exploring the concept of bug bounties, their history, and the various benefits they offer to both researchers and organizations. From there, we'll dive into the practical aspects, discussing the essential techniques used in bug hunting, the tools you'll need, and the methodologies that will set you apart from the crowd.

But bug hunting isn't just about technical skills. Throughout this book, we'll also explore the mindset and attributes necessary for success. I'll share the lessons I've learned along the way, including the importance of persistence, continuous learning, and adapting to the ever-changing landscape of cybersecurity.

As we progress, you'll discover strategies for maximizing your earnings, selecting the right bug bounty platforms, and effectively managing your relationships with organizations. We'll delve into real-life case studies, examining successful bug reports and analyzing the impact they had on the companies involved.

Ethics and responsible disclosure are fundamental principles we'll cover extensively. We'll discuss the legal considerations surrounding bug bounties, along with the ethical dilemmas that may arise, helping you navigate this field with integrity and professionalism.

In addition to personal growth, we'll explore the opportunities for career advancement within the bug bounty community. From transitioning to full-time bug hunting to establishing your personal brand, this book will provide insights and strategies to help you make the most of your bug bounty journey.

Lastly, we'll delve into the thriving bug bounty community itself. I'll highlight the importance of engaging with fellow researchers, participating in events and conferences, and contributing back to the community that has given us so much.

Bug bounty hunting is an exciting and dynamic field, filled with endless opportunities for growth and learning. Whether you aspire to become a top earner, gain recognition, or simply sharpen your cybersecurity skills, this book will be your comprehensive guide to achieving bug bounty success.

Get ready to embark on an adventure that will challenge you, expand your knowledge, and unlock the secrets to becoming a top earner in the bug bounty community. Let's dive in!

Chapter 1: Introduction to Bug Bounty Programs

Welcome to Chapter 1 of "Bug Bounty Success: How to Become a Top Earner in the Bug Bounty Community." In this chapter, we will dive into the fascinating world of bug bounty programs and lay the foundation for your journey as a bug bounty hunter.

Bug bounty programs have revolutionized the way organizations approach cybersecurity. They offer a unique opportunity for talented individuals like you to uncover vulnerabilities in digital systems and help companies fortify their defenses. In this chapter, we will explore the concept of bug bounties, their evolution, and the myriad benefits they provide to both researchers and organizations.

We'll start by defining what bug bounty programs are and how they differ from traditional security testing methods. Understanding the distinct characteristics and principles of bug bounties will set the stage for your success in this field.

Additionally, we will delve into the historical overview of bug bounty programs, tracing their roots and examining how they have grown into integral components of modern cybersecurity strategies. By understanding the evolution of bug bounties, you will gain insights into the current landscape and the opportunities that lie ahead.

Throughout this chapter, we will also explore the many benefits of participating in bug bounty programs. From financial rewards and recognition to valuable learning experiences and networking opportunities, bug bounties offer a range of advantages for both aspiring and experienced bug bounty hunters.

By the end of this chapter, you will have a solid understanding of the fundamentals of bug bounty programs, their historical context, and the wide-ranging benefits they offer. This knowledge will serve as the bedrock for your bug hunting journey, setting you up for success as you progress through the rest of this book.

Get ready to unlock the secrets of bug bounty success and embark on a thrilling adventure in the realm of cybersecurity. Let's begin our exploration of bug bounty programs and discover how you can become a top earner in the bug bounty community.

1.1 What Are Bug Bounty Programs?

Bug bounty programs have emerged as an innovative approach to cybersecurity, leveraging the power of crowdsourcing to identify and address vulnerabilities in digital systems. In this section, we will delve into the concept of bug bounty programs, exploring their purpose, mechanics, and benefits.

Bug bounty programs are initiatives launched by organizations to invite external security researchers, commonly known as bug bounty hunters, to discover and report vulnerabilities in their software, websites, or applications. These programs aim to harness the collective intelligence and diverse skillsets of the security community to enhance the overall security posture of the organization.

The mechanics of bug bounty programs are relatively straightforward. Organizations establish clear guidelines and rules, outlining the scope of the program, the types of vulnerabilities they are interested in, and the rewards offered for valid bug reports. Bug bounty hunters are then invited to actively search for vulnerabilities within the defined scope, with the goal of responsibly disclosing any findings to the organization.

One of the primary benefits of bug bounty programs is their ability to tap into a vast network of security researchers from around the world. By opening their systems to external scrutiny, organizations gain access to a diverse talent pool that can bring fresh perspectives and uncover vulnerabilities that may have been missed during internal security assessments.

Bug bounty programs offer several advantages compared to traditional penetration testing or vulnerability scanning. Traditional methods typically involve a limited number of security experts conducting assessments within a specific timeframe. In contrast, bug bounty programs provide continuous testing, allowing organizations to benefit from ongoing vulnerability discovery as new researchers join the program or existing participants expand their efforts.

Bug bounty programs also offer a cost-effective approach to security testing. Instead of relying solely on in-house security teams or hiring external experts for short-term engagements, organizations pay only for the valid bug reports they receive. This pay-for-results model aligns incentives, encouraging bug bounty hunters to invest time and effort in discovering impactful vulnerabilities.

Furthermore, bug bounty programs foster a culture of collaboration and knowledge sharing within the cybersecurity community. By providing platforms for bug bounty hunters to interact, share insights, and learn from one another, these programs enable the collective growth and development of the bug hunting community. Bug bounty hunters can exchange techniques, discuss emerging attack vectors, and collectively raise the bar for digital security.

Bug bounty programs also contribute to responsible disclosure practices. By establishing clear guidelines and communication channels, organizations encourage bug bounty hunters to disclose vulnerabilities directly to them, giving them an opportunity to address the issues before they can be exploited maliciously. This responsible disclosure process helps organizations avoid potential reputational damage and financial losses that could arise from public exposure of unaddressed vulnerabilities.

Organizations that embrace bug bounty programs benefit from improved security resilience. By actively seeking out vulnerabilities and addressing them promptly, organizations can proactively fortify their defenses and reduce the likelihood of successful cyber attacks. This proactive approach to security reinforces trust and confidence among customers, stakeholders, and the wider public.

Bug bounty programs have gained significant traction across various industries, with both tech giants and small startups adopting them as part of their cybersecurity strategies. Tech companies such as Google, Microsoft, and Facebook have pioneered bug bounty programs and have seen tremendous success in identifying and addressing vulnerabilities through the participation of skilled researchers.

In conclusion, bug bounty programs offer a unique and effective approach to cybersecurity by leveraging the collective intelligence and expertise of the global security community. These programs enable organizations to harness external talent, continuously test their systems for vulnerabilities, and improve their overall security posture. With their cost-effectiveness, responsible disclosure practices, and fostering of collaboration, bug bounty programs are poised to continue evolving and play a significant role in the ongoing battle against cyber threats.

1.2 Historical Overview of Bug Bounties

Bug bounties have a rich history that traces back several decades. In this section, we will provide a historical overview of bug bounties, highlighting significant milestones and the evolution of these programs over time.

The concept of bug bounties can be traced back to the early 1990s when technology companies started recognizing the value of external contributions in identifying and fixing software vulnerabilities. In 1995, the first known bug bounty program, known as the Netscape Bug Bounty Program, was launched by Netscape Communications Corporation. The program offered cash rewards to individuals who reported security bugs in their Netscape Navigator web browser.

During the late 1990s and early 2000s, bug bounty programs gained further momentum as open-source software projects, such as the Apache HTTP Server and the Mozilla Foundation, began to offer incentives for discovering and reporting vulnerabilities. These early initiatives helped shape the foundations of bug bounty programs by fostering a culture of collaboration and incentivizing security researchers to contribute their expertise.

In 2004, the organization iDefense (now part of Accenture) launched the Vulnerability Contributor Program (VCP), which provided monetary rewards for vulnerability submissions. The VCP established a formal structure for incentivizing researchers to report vulnerabilities, further solidifying the concept of bug bounties.

The modern bug bounty landscape began to take shape in the late 2000s with the introduction of dedicated bug bounty platforms. In 2007, the platform HackerOne (originally known as "Mikko's Bug Bounty") was launched, offering a centralized platform for organizations to engage with security researchers and manage their bug bounty programs. HackerOne played a pivotal role in popularizing bug bounties and making them more accessible to organizations of all sizes.

In 2010, Facebook made headlines by launching its own bug bounty program, becoming one of the first major tech companies to offer significant financial rewards for security bug reports. This move signaled a shift in the industry, with other prominent companies following suit and adopting bug bounty programs as an integral part of their security strategies.

Bug bounty programs continued to gain traction and visibility throughout the 2010s. Companies like Google, Microsoft, and Apple established highly successful bug bounty programs, attracting talented security researchers from around the world. The increasing participation and impact of bug bounty hunters led to the discovery of critical vulnerabilities in widely-used software and online platforms, further highlighting the value of bug bounties in enhancing digital security.

In recent years, bug bounty programs have evolved and diversified. Organizations across various industries, including finance, healthcare, and automotive, have embraced bug bounties as an effective means of bolstering their security defenses. Governments and non-profit organizations have also launched bug bounty programs to address vulnerabilities in critical infrastructure and public-facing services.

The scope of bug bounty programs has expanded beyond traditional software and web applications. Bug bounties now cover areas such as mobile applications, IoT devices, blockchain platforms, and even physical hardware. This broadening scope reflects the growing complexity of the digital landscape and the need for comprehensive security testing across a wide range of technologies.

As bug bounty programs have matured, best practices and ethical guidelines have emerged to ensure responsible and effective engagement between organizations and bug bounty hunters. Platforms like HackerOne, Bugcrowd, and Synack provide the infrastructure and support for bug bounty programs, facilitating collaboration, secure vulnerability reporting, and fair reward distribution.

Looking to the future, bug bounties are expected to continue to thrive and evolve alongside advancements in technology and cybersecurity. The integration of automation and AI-powered tools into bug bounty platforms will streamline vulnerability detection and analysis. Greater collaboration and information sharing within the bug bounty community will lead to the discovery of more complex and systemic vulnerabilities. The ongoing growth of bug bounty programs will contribute to a more secure digital ecosystem, with organizations and researchers working together to address emerging threats.

In conclusion, bug bounties have come a long way since their inception, evolving from informal initiatives to organized and structured programs. They have become an integral part of the cybersecurity landscape, providing a platform for organizations to tap into external talent and enhance their security posture. As bug bounty programs continue to mature and adapt to emerging challenges, they will play an increasingly critical role in strengthening the security of digital systems and fostering collaboration within the cybersecurity community.

1.3 Benefits of Participating in Bug Bounties

Participating in bug bounties offers numerous benefits for security researchers, also known as bug bounty hunters. In this section, we will explore the advantages and rewards of engaging in bug bounty programs.

Financial Rewards: Bug bounties provide an opportunity for bug bounty hunters to earn financial rewards for their skills and expertise. Successful bug reports that uncover critical vulnerabilities can result in substantial monetary payouts. These rewards can range from a few hundred dollars to tens of thousands of dollars, depending on the severity and impact of the reported vulnerability. For talented and dedicated bug hunters, bug bounties can serve as a lucrative source of income.

Skill Development: Bug bounty programs offer a practical and hands-on learning environment for security researchers. By actively searching for vulnerabilities and analyzing systems, bug bounty hunters gain valuable experience in identifying security weaknesses and understanding different attack vectors. The continuous exposure to real-world scenarios hones their skills in vulnerability discovery, exploit development, and secure coding practices. Bug bounties provide an excellent platform for skill development and growth within the cybersecurity field.

Recognition and Reputation: Participating in bug bounties allows researchers to showcase their expertise and build a reputation within the cybersecurity community. Reporting valid and impactful vulnerabilities establishes credibility and earns the respect of peers and industry professionals. A track record of successful bug reports can lead to recognition from organizations, bug bounty platforms, and the wider community. Bug bounty hunters who consistently deliver high-quality reports and demonstrate ethical conduct can establish themselves as trusted experts in the field.

Networking and Collaboration: Bug bounty programs provide opportunities for bug bounty hunters to network and collaborate with fellow researchers, organizations, and industry experts. Engaging in bug bounties exposes participants to a diverse community of like-minded professionals, creating avenues for knowledge sharing, idea exchange, and collaboration on complex vulnerabilities. Building connections within the bug bounty community can lead to mentorship opportunities, career growth, and partnerships for future security research endeavors.

Continuous Learning: Bug bounties offer an environment that fosters continuous learning. The evolving nature of cybersecurity requires bug bounty hunters to stay updated with the latest attack techniques, emerging technologies, and defensive strategies. Engaging in bug bounties exposes researchers to diverse systems, frameworks, and platforms, providing valuable insights and hands-on experience. The constant challenges and exposure to different vulnerabilities enhance bug bounty hunters' ability to adapt, learn new techniques, and stay at the forefront of the cybersecurity landscape.

Contributing to Digital Security: Participating in bug bounties allows researchers to make a tangible and positive impact on the security of digital systems. By uncovering and reporting vulnerabilities, bug bounty hunters help organizations identify and address weaknesses before they can be exploited by malicious actors. This proactive approach to security contributes to the overall resilience of digital infrastructure and helps protect individuals, businesses, and critical services from cyber threats. Bug bounty hunters play a vital role in improving the security posture of organizations and the broader digital ecosystem.

Personal and Professional Growth: Engaging in bug bounties offers personal and professional growth opportunities. The challenges, successes, and lessons learned during bug hunting journeys contribute to personal development, resilience, and problem-solving skills. Bug bounty hunters gain insights into the intricacies of cybersecurity, develop analytical thinking, and enhance their ability to assess risk and identify vulnerabilities. Additionally, the reputation and recognition gained through bug bounty participation can open doors to career advancement, job opportunities, and speaking engagements within the cybersecurity industry.

In conclusion, participating in bug bounties provides numerous benefits for security researchers. From financial rewards to skill development, recognition, networking, continuous learning, and contributing to digital security, bug bounty programs offer a unique and rewarding experience. Bug bounty hunters who actively engage in these programs can leverage the opportunities to grow their expertise, build their reputation, and make a significant impact on the cybersecurity landscape.

Chapter 2: Getting Started in Bug Bounties

Welcome to Chapter 2 of "Bug Bounty Success: How to Become a Top Earner in the Bug Bounty Community." In this chapter, we will guide you through the essential steps to kickstart your bug bounty journey and set yourself up for success.

Getting started in bug bounties requires careful preparation and a solid understanding of the key elements involved. In this chapter, we will explore the foundational aspects that will help you establish a strong foothold in the bug bounty community.

We will begin by building your bug bounty toolkit. We'll discuss the essential tools, software, and hardware that will aid you in your bug hunting endeavors. From vulnerability scanners and proxy tools to virtual machines and debugging software, we'll cover the necessary resources that every bug bounty hunter should have at their disposal.

Next, we'll dive into selecting bug bounty platforms and programs. With numerous platforms available, it's important to understand their features, rewards, and the types of vulnerabilities they focus on. We'll provide insights on choosing the right platforms that align with your skills and interests, maximizing your chances of finding impactful bugs and earning substantial rewards.

Understanding the rules and guidelines of bug bounty programs is vital to ensure a smooth and successful bug hunting experience. We'll explore the common guidelines set by organizations, such as responsible disclosure policies, scope limitations, and rules for reporting vulnerabilities. By familiarizing yourself with these guidelines, you'll avoid potential pitfalls and navigate bug bounty programs with professionalism and efficiency.

As we wrap up this chapter, you'll have a well-equipped bug bounty toolkit, a clear understanding of the platforms and programs available, and the knowledge to navigate the rules and guidelines of bug bounty hunting. Armed with this information, you'll be ready to embark on your bug hunting journey with confidence and maximize your chances of success.

Prepare yourself for the exciting challenges that lie ahead as we delve deeper into the intricacies of bug bounty hunting. In the following chapters, we'll explore essential bug hunting techniques, mindset development, maximizing your earnings, and much more. Let's continue our quest to becoming a top earner in the bug bounty community.

2.1 Building Your Bug Bounty Toolkit

Building a comprehensive bug bounty toolkit is essential for bug bounty hunters seeking success in discovering and reporting vulnerabilities. In this section, we will explore the key components that make up an effective bug bounty toolkit.

Virtual Machines and Operating Systems: Bug bounty hunters often require a variety of virtual machines (VMs) and operating systems (OS) to test and analyze different software and environments. VMs allow for isolation and easy setup of testing environments, while diverse OS options enable compatibility testing across platforms. Common VM solutions include VirtualBox, VMware, and Docker, while popular OS choices include Linux distributions (such as Kali Linux and Ubuntu) and Windows.

Web Application Testing Tools: Web applications are a prime target for bug bounty hunters, so having a range of web application testing tools is crucial. These tools aid in discovering common vulnerabilities such as cross-site scripting (XSS), SQL injection, and insecure direct object references. Some popular web application testing tools include Burp Suite, OWASP ZAP, Nikto, and Nmap. These tools help automate parts of the testing process and streamline vulnerability identification.

Network Scanners and Reconnaissance Tools: Network scanning and reconnaissance tools assist in mapping out network infrastructure, identifying open ports, and gathering information about potential targets. Tools like Nmap, Masscan, and Shodan enable bug bounty hunters to discover exposed services, determine the attack surface, and gather valuable intelligence for vulnerability analysis.

Fuzzing Tools: Fuzzing involves sending unexpected and malformed input to software applications to uncover vulnerabilities. Fuzzing tools generate large volumes of test inputs, systematically probing an application for unexpected behavior. Popular fuzzing tools include American Fuzzy Lop (AFL), Peach Fuzzer, and OWASP ZAP's active scanner. Fuzzing can be highly effective in identifying vulnerabilities, particularly in complex and less-tested code.

Exploit Development Frameworks: Exploitation frameworks are essential for advanced bug bounty hunters who delve into vulnerability exploitation and proof-of-concept (PoC) development. Frameworks like Metasploit, ExploitDB, and the Social-Engineer Toolkit (SET) provide a vast array of exploits, payloads, and post-exploitation modules. These frameworks help automate the process of building and testing exploits against known vulnerabilities.

Code Analysis and Reverse Engineering Tools: Understanding how software works at a code level can help bug bounty hunters identify vulnerabilities that may not be evident through traditional testing techniques. Tools like IDA Pro, Ghidra, and Radare2 assist in analyzing binary code, decompiling executables, and reverse engineering applications. These tools are particularly useful when examining closed-source software or proprietary protocols.

Secure Coding Resources: Familiarity with secure coding practices is vital for bug bounty hunters to identify vulnerabilities and provide actionable recommendations to developers. Resources such as the OWASP Top 10, the Web Application Security Consortium (WASC) Threat Classification, and secure coding guidelines from various programming languages help bug bounty hunters understand common pitfalls and suggest remediation steps.

Reporting Templates and Documentation: Clear and concise bug reports are essential for effective communication with organizations. Having well-structured reporting templates and documentation helps bug bounty hunters provide detailed information about vulnerabilities, including the steps to reproduce, potential impact, and suggested fixes. Templates can be customized based on bug bounty program requirements and help streamline the reporting process.

Learning Resources and Communities: Continuous learning is fundamental to success in bug bounties.

Bug bounty hunters should have access to resources such as blogs, forums, online courses, and communities where they can learn from others, share knowledge, and stay updated with the latest security trends. Platforms like Bugcrowd, HackerOne, and the r/bugbounty subreddit offer valuable resources, discussions, and opportunities to engage with the bug bounty community.

Networking and Collaboration Channels: Building connections within the bug bounty community provides invaluable opportunities for collaboration, mentorship, and knowledge sharing. Networking channels, such as bug bounty platforms' chat rooms, Discord servers, or dedicated bug bounty forums, allow bug bounty hunters to connect with like-minded individuals, share experiences, and benefit from collective expertise.

As the bug bounty landscape evolves, bug bounty hunters must continuously evaluate and update their toolkit. Regularly exploring new tools, techniques, and frameworks helps bug bounty hunters stay effective, efficient, and adaptable in their bug hunting endeavors.

Building a comprehensive bug bounty toolkit is an ongoing process that requires research, experimentation, and a willingness to adapt to emerging trends and technologies. By investing in the right tools and resources, bug bounty hunters can increase their chances of discovering impactful vulnerabilities and contributing to the improvement of digital security.

2.2 Selecting Bug Bounty Platforms and Programs

When participating in bug bounties, selecting the right bug bounty platforms and programs is crucial for maximizing your chances of success. In this section, we will explore key factors to consider when choosing bug bounty platforms and programs to ensure a productive and rewarding bug hunting experience.

Reputation and Credibility: Start by evaluating the reputation and credibility of bug bounty platforms and programs. Research the track record of the platform or program in terms of the number of active programs, the quality of reported vulnerabilities, and the responsiveness of the platform to bug reports. Look for platforms that have established themselves as trusted entities within the bug bounty community and have a solid reputation for fair and timely rewards.

Program Scope and Diversity: Assess the program scope and diversity offered by bug bounty platforms. Look for platforms that host a wide range of programs spanning various industries and technologies. A diverse selection of programs allows bug bounty hunters to explore different domains, expand their knowledge, and engage with organizations that align with their interests and expertise.

Reward Structure: Examine the reward structure of bug bounty programs to ensure it aligns with your expectations and goals. Look for programs that offer competitive and fair rewards based on the severity and impact of the reported vulnerabilities. Consider the average payout amounts, bonuses for critical vulnerabilities, and the transparency of the reward calculation process. It's essential to have a clear understanding of the financial incentives provided by the bug bounty program.

Program Transparency: Evaluate the transparency of bug bounty programs in terms of their rules, guidelines, and expectations. Transparent programs clearly define their scope, acceptable testing methodologies, and eligible targets. Look for programs that provide detailed instructions on vulnerability reporting, communication channels, and expected response times. Transparency helps avoid ambiguity and ensures a smooth bug reporting and reward process.

Communication and Support: Consider the level of communication and support provided by bug bounty platforms and programs. Look for platforms that offer responsive support, maintain active communication channels, and provide bug bounty hunters with timely updates on the status of their reports. Platforms that facilitate effective communication between bug hunters and program owners can help resolve any questions or issues that may arise during the bug hunting process.

Platform Tools and Features: Evaluate the tools and features offered by bug bounty platforms to facilitate bug hunting. Look for platforms that provide integrated vulnerability submission forms, vulnerability tracking dashboards, and bug report management systems. These features can streamline the bug reporting process, enable better tracking of reported vulnerabilities, and improve the overall bug hunting experience.

Community Engagement: Consider the level of community engagement facilitated by bug bounty platforms. Look for platforms that provide avenues for bug bounty hunters to engage with each other, share knowledge, and seek advice. Features like chat rooms, forums, and mentorship programs foster collaboration, enhance learning, and offer opportunities to network with fellow bug bounty hunters.

Legal and Ethical Considerations: Ensure that bug bounty platforms and programs have clear legal and ethical guidelines in place. Look for platforms that promote responsible disclosure practices, protect bug hunters from legal repercussions, and facilitate ethical bug hunting. Consider the platform's stance on disclosing vulnerabilities responsibly, engaging in coordinated disclosure, and protecting the interests of both bug hunters and program owners.

Payment and Rewards Process: Review the payment and rewards process of bug bounty platforms. Look for platforms that offer efficient and timely payment processes, ensuring that bug bounty hunters receive their rewards promptly. Consider the available payment options, such as bank transfers or cryptocurrency, and evaluate the platform's track record in honoring and processing rewards.

User Feedback and Reviews: Finally, seek out user feedback and reviews from other bug bounty hunters who have participated in bug bounty programs on the platform. Their insights and experiences can provide valuable information about the platform's strengths, weaknesses, and overall user satisfaction. Consider joining bug bounty community forums or social media groups to gather firsthand feedback from experienced bug hunters.

By carefully considering these factors, you can select bug bounty platforms and programs that align with your goals, provide a conducive bug hunting environment, and offer fair rewards. Remember, finding the right bug bounty platforms and programs enhances your chances of discovering valuable vulnerabilities, building your reputation, and maximizing the benefits of your bug hunting efforts.

2.3 Understanding Rules and Guidelines

Understanding the rules and guidelines of bug bounty programs is crucial for bug bounty hunters to ensure a smooth and successful bug hunting experience. In this section, we will explore key aspects of bug bounty rules and guidelines that bug bounty hunters should familiarize themselves with.

Scope of the Program: The scope of a bug bounty program defines the boundaries within which bug bounty hunters can conduct their testing. It specifies the systems, applications, websites, or assets that are in-scope and eligible for bug hunting. Understanding the scope helps bug bounty hunters focus their efforts on relevant targets and avoid wasting time on out-of-scope areas.

Testing Methodologies: Bug bounty programs may have specific guidelines on acceptable testing methodologies. It's important to understand what types of testing are allowed and what activities are prohibited. For example, programs may specify whether automated scanning tools, social engineering techniques, or denial-of-service attacks are permitted or restricted. Adhering to the specified testing methodologies ensures bug hunters stay within the program's guidelines.

Vulnerability Types: Bug bounty programs often define the types of vulnerabilities they are interested in. These may include common vulnerabilities such as cross-site scripting (XSS), SQL injection, remote code execution (RCE), or authentication bypass. Familiarize yourself with the program's preferred vulnerability types to align your bug hunting efforts with their priorities.

Disclosure and Reporting Requirements: Bug bounty programs have specific requirements for vulnerability disclosure and reporting. Understand how vulnerabilities should be reported, which communication channels to use, and what information should be included in the bug report. Some programs may require proof-of-concept (PoC) code, while others may specify specific report templates or formats. Adhering to the reporting requirements ensures that your bug reports are submitted correctly and promptly.

Exclusions and Limitations: Bug bounty programs may have exclusions and limitations that bug bounty hunters need to be aware of. These can include restrictions on testing third-party applications, explicit exclusions of specific systems or components, or limitations on the number of submissions per day.

Understanding these exclusions and limitations helps bug hunters avoid wasting time on ineligible targets and ensures compliance with program rules.

Coordinated Disclosure: Bug bounty programs often emphasize responsible and coordinated disclosure of vulnerabilities. Understand the program's policy on disclosure timelines and whether they require a period of confidentiality to allow the organization to fix the vulnerability before it is made public. Adhering to the program's disclosure policies helps maintain a positive and ethical bug hunting practice.

Communication Channels: Bug bounty programs specify the channels through which bug hunters should communicate with program owners or coordinators. These channels may include email addresses, chat platforms, or dedicated bug bounty platform communication features. Familiarize yourself with the designated communication channels to ensure efficient and effective communication during the bug hunting process.

Rules on Data Privacy and Legal Compliance: Bug bounty programs often have rules and guidelines regarding data privacy and legal compliance. These may include instructions on handling sensitive data, rules against accessing or tampering with user data, or restrictions on conducting activities that violate laws or regulations. It's essential to respect privacy and legal boundaries while conducting bug hunting activities.

Duplicate Submissions: Bug bounty programs typically address the issue of duplicate submissions, where multiple bug hunters report the same vulnerability. Understand the program's policy on duplicate reports, whether they honor the first report or have a specific process for handling duplicates. Some programs may offer partial rewards for duplicates, while others may exclude duplicates from the reward process.

Rewards and Payouts: Finally, understand the program's reward structure and payout process. This includes information on the types of vulnerabilities eligible for rewards, the severity levels associated with different vulnerabilities, and the payment timelines or processes. Familiarize yourself with the program's reward guidelines to have clarity on the potential financial benefits of your bug hunting efforts.

By thoroughly understanding the rules and guidelines of bug bounty programs, bug bounty hunters can align their activities with program expectations, avoid potential pitfalls, and ensure a positive bug hunting experience. Adhering to these guidelines not only helps maintain a productive relationship with the program owners but also contributes to responsible and ethical bug hunting practices.

Chapter 3: Essential Bug Hunting Techniques

Welcome to Chapter 3 of "Bug Bounty Success: How to Become a Top Earner in the Bug Bounty Community." In this chapter, we will delve into the essential bug hunting techniques that will sharpen your skills and empower you to uncover vulnerabilities effectively.

Bug hunting is both an art and a science, requiring a combination of technical expertise, critical thinking, and creativity. In this chapter, we will explore the fundamental techniques that successful bug bounty hunters employ to identify and exploit vulnerabilities.

We'll begin by discussing the crucial phase of reconnaissance and information gathering. You'll learn how to gather valuable intelligence about your target, including understanding its architecture, technologies used, and potential attack vectors. We'll explore techniques such as open-source intelligence (OSINT) gathering, subdomain enumeration, and analyzing application behavior to gain a comprehensive understanding of your target's digital presence.

Next, we'll dive into the identification of common vulnerabilities and weaknesses. We'll cover the OWASP Top 10 vulnerabilities, such as cross-site scripting (XSS), SQL injection, and insecure direct object references. You'll learn how to detect and exploit these vulnerabilities effectively, using both manual and automated techniques.

Exploiting and validating discovered bugs is the next critical step in the bug hunting process. We'll explore methodologies and tools for exploiting vulnerabilities, validating their impact, and crafting impactful proof-of-concept demonstrations. You'll gain insights into various techniques, such as privilege escalation, remote code execution, and bypassing security controls, to demonstrate the severity and impact of discovered vulnerabilities.

Throughout this chapter, we'll emphasize the importance of continuous learning and staying up to date with the latest attack techniques and defensive measures. Bug hunting is an ever-evolving field, and being proactive in expanding your knowledge is crucial for success.

By the end of this chapter, you'll have a strong foundation in essential bug hunting techniques. You'll be equipped with the skills to gather critical information, identify common vulnerabilities, and exploit and validate discovered bugs. These techniques will serve as powerful tools in your bug hunting arsenal as we progress further into the intricacies of becoming a top earner in the bug bounty community.

Get ready to hone your bug hunting skills and unlock the secrets to uncovering high-impact vulnerabilities. In the following chapters, we'll delve into mindset development, maximizing your bug bounty earnings, and effectively navigating bug bounty platforms. Let's continue our quest for bug bounty success together.

3.1 Reconnaissance and Information Gathering

Reconnaissance and information gathering are crucial initial steps in bug bounty hunting. These processes involve gathering relevant data and intelligence about the target systems, applications, or organizations. In this section, we will explore key techniques and tools used for reconnaissance and information gathering in bug bounty hunting.

Passive Information Gathering: Passive information gathering involves collecting publicly available information about the target without directly interacting with its systems. This includes conducting searches on search engines, social media platforms, and public code repositories to gather information such as employee names, email addresses, domain names, technology stack, subdomains, and related websites. Tools like Google, Shodan, and GitHub can be utilized to discover valuable data passively.

Active Information Gathering: Active information gathering involves actively interacting with the target systems to collect information. Techniques like port scanning, banner grabbing, and network mapping can help identify open ports, exposed services, and network infrastructure. Tools like Nmap, Masscan, and Shodan assist in actively scanning the target network and gathering insights on potential attack vectors.

Subdomain Enumeration: Subdomain enumeration helps identify subdomains associated with the target domain. By discovering subdomains, bug bounty hunters can expand their attack surface and uncover potential vulnerabilities. Tools like Sublist3r, Amass, and KnockPy can automate the process of subdomain enumeration, allowing bug hunters to gather a comprehensive list of subdomains for further analysis.

DNS Analysis: Analyzing the Domain Name System (DNS) records can provide valuable information about the target's infrastructure and third-party services. By examining DNS records, bug bounty hunters can identify mail servers, content delivery networks (CDNs), and other external services that may be in scope. Tools like dig, dnsrecon, and dnswalk aid in DNS analysis, allowing bug hunters to extract useful data from DNS records.

Web Technology Identification: Understanding the technologies used by the target web application can provide insights into potential vulnerabilities or misconfigurations. Tools like Wappalyzer, BuiltWith, and WhatWeb assist in identifying web technologies, frameworks, CMS platforms, and server software employed by the target. This information helps bug bounty hunters focus their testing efforts on relevant vulnerabilities.

Social Engineering and OSINT: Open Source Intelligence (OSINT) techniques involve gathering information from publicly available sources to build a comprehensive profile of the target. This includes searching for employee profiles on professional networking platforms, exploring public forums or mailing lists for discussions related to the target, and analyzing any leaked information or data breaches associated with the target organization. Social engineering techniques can help gather additional information by engaging with individuals associated with the target.

Content Discovery and Crawling: Content discovery and web crawling tools enable bug bounty hunters to identify hidden or forgotten web pages, directories, and files on the target website. These tools explore the target website's structure, identify potential entry points, and discover pages that may have been unintentionally exposed. Tools like Dirsearch,

Gobuster, and Burp Suite's Spider functionality assist in content discovery and crawling.

Bug Bounty Platform Reports: If the bug bounty program is hosted on a bug bounty platform, bug hunters can review previous bug reports and vulnerabilities disclosed by other researchers. This can provide insights into common vulnerabilities, testing methodologies, and potential attack vectors relevant to the target. Analyzing the platform's disclosed reports helps bug hunters avoid duplicates and focus on unexplored areas.

Remember to respect legal and ethical boundaries when conducting reconnaissance and information gathering. Ensure that the techniques used comply with the bug bounty program's rules and guidelines, as well as any applicable laws or regulations. The gathered information should be used solely for bug hunting purposes and not for malicious activities.

Reconnaissance and information gathering lay the foundation for successful bug bounty hunting. By diligently collecting and analyzing relevant data, bug bounty hunters can uncover potential attack vectors, identify weak points in the target's security posture, and focus their efforts on areas likely to yield vulnerabilities.

3.2 Identifying Common Vulnerabilities and Weaknesses

Identifying common vulnerabilities and weaknesses is a crucial step in bug bounty hunting. By understanding and recognizing these vulnerabilities, bug bounty hunters can focus their testing efforts and increase the likelihood of discovering impactful security flaws. In this section, we will explore some of the most common vulnerabilities and weaknesses targeted during bug bounty hunting.

Cross-Site Scripting (XSS): XSS vulnerabilities occur when an attacker injects malicious code (usually JavaScript) into a web application, which is then executed by the victim's browser. XSS vulnerabilities can allow attackers to steal sensitive information, perform session hijacking, or even take control of user accounts. Bug bounty hunters should test for both reflected XSS (where the payload is embedded in the response) and stored XSS (where the payload is permanently stored on the server).

SQL Injection: SQL injection vulnerabilities occur when an attacker can manipulate SQL queries executed by a web application's database. By injecting malicious SQL code, attackers can manipulate the database, extract sensitive information, or even execute arbitrary commands. Bug bounty hunters should test for SQL injection by attempting to insert malicious input into user-controlled SQL queries and analyzing the application's response.

Server-Side Request Forgery (SSRF): SSRF vulnerabilities allow attackers to make requests from the server to arbitrary external resources. By manipulating the server's requests, attackers can potentially access internal resources, bypass firewall restrictions, or perform attacks on internal systems. Bug bounty hunters should test for SSRF by manipulating server-side requests and analyzing the application's responses for potential vulnerabilities.

Remote Code Execution (RCE): RCE vulnerabilities enable attackers to execute arbitrary code on the target system or server. These vulnerabilities are typically severe and can lead to complete compromise of the target. Bug bounty hunters should test for RCE by looking for input validation or deserialization issues that could allow for remote code execution.

Authentication and Session Management Issues: Authentication and session management vulnerabilities can lead to unauthorized access or session hijacking. Bug bounty hunters should test for weak passwords, inadequate session expiration or management, predictable session IDs, insecure password reset mechanisms, and other authentication-related weaknesses.

Cross-Site Request Forgery (CSRF): CSRF vulnerabilities occur when an attacker tricks a victim into performing unintended actions on a website where the victim is authenticated. By leveraging the victim's authenticated session, attackers can perform actions on behalf of the victim, potentially leading to unauthorized actions or data manipulation. Bug bounty hunters should test for CSRF vulnerabilities by attempting to manipulate requests and observe the application's response.

Insecure Direct Object References (IDOR): IDOR vulnerabilities occur when an application exposes direct references to internal objects, such as database records or file paths, without proper authorization checks. Attackers can manipulate these references to gain unauthorized access to sensitive data or perform actions they should not have access to. Bug bounty hunters should test for IDOR by attempting to access objects or data that they shouldn't be able to access.

Server Misconfigurations: Misconfigurations in servers, services, or infrastructure can lead to significant vulnerabilities. These can include exposed sensitive information, open ports, outdated software, default credentials, or weak security settings. Bug bounty hunters should examine server configurations and perform reconnaissance to identify potential misconfigurations that could lead to security weaknesses.

Information Disclosure: Information disclosure vulnerabilities occur when an application reveals sensitive information unintentionally. This can include disclosing internal file paths, error messages, stack traces, or credentials. Bug bounty hunters should analyze the application's responses and error messages to identify any instances where sensitive information is exposed.

Business Logic Flaws: Business logic flaws are vulnerabilities that arise from flaws or weaknesses in the application's logic and processes. These vulnerabilities can enable attackers to bypass authorization, perform unauthorized actions, or manipulate workflows to their advantage. Bug bounty hunters should thoroughly understand the application's intended behavior and test for deviations or flaws in its business logic.

Bug bounty hunters should leverage various tools and techniques to identify these vulnerabilities, including manual testing, automated scanning tools, fuzzing, code review, and security testing frameworks. It's important to follow the rules and guidelines of the bug bounty program and communicate any identified vulnerabilities effectively to the program owners.

By focusing on these common vulnerabilities and weaknesses, bug bounty hunters can increase their chances of discovering impactful security flaws, earning valuable rewards, and contributing to the overall improvement of digital security.

3.3 Exploiting and Validating Discovered Bugs

Once a bug has been discovered during bug bounty hunting, the next step is to exploit and validate the vulnerability to demonstrate its impact and severity. Exploiting and validating discovered bugs helps bug bounty hunters provide actionable evidence to program owners and ensure that the reported vulnerability is valid and exploitable. In this section, we will explore the process of exploiting and validating discovered bugs.

Understanding the Vulnerability: Before attempting to exploit a discovered bug, bug bounty hunters should have a thorough understanding of the vulnerability and its underlying cause. Analyze the nature of the vulnerability, its impact, and the potential attack vectors it presents. This understanding will guide the exploitation process and help determine the most effective approach.

Setting Up a Test Environment: It is crucial to set up a controlled and isolated test environment to exploit the vulnerability. This ensures that any unintended consequences or impact on production systems is avoided. Create a dedicated testing environment that replicates the target system, including the necessary software versions, configurations, and dependencies.

Developing an Exploit or Proof-of-Concept (PoC): Depending on the nature of the vulnerability, bug bounty hunters may need to develop an exploit or a proof-of-concept (PoC) to demonstrate the vulnerability's impact. An exploit takes advantage of the vulnerability to gain unauthorized access, execute arbitrary code, or perform other malicious actions. A PoC demonstrates the vulnerability without causing harm, providing a controlled way to validate the bug's existence and severity. Care should be taken to ensure that the exploit or PoC does not cause unintended damage or violate any laws or regulations.

Exploitation Techniques: Exploiting a discovered bug requires applying appropriate techniques based on the vulnerability's nature and the target system. This can involve injecting malicious payloads, manipulating input fields, bypassing authentication mechanisms, or executing unauthorized commands. Bug bounty hunters may utilize various tools, scripting languages, or frameworks to aid in the exploitation process. It is essential to conduct exploitation in a controlled manner to avoid any unintended consequences or collateral damage.

Capturing and Documenting Evidence: During the exploitation process, it is crucial to capture evidence that clearly demonstrates the vulnerability's impact and severity. This evidence serves as proof for the bug bounty program owners to validate the reported vulnerability. Capture screenshots, videos, logs, or any other relevant artifacts that clearly showcase the exploit in action. Detailed documentation of the steps taken during the exploitation process ensures a clear and concise report submission.

Testing Variations and Edge Cases: While validating a discovered bug, it is important to test different variations and edge cases to determine the scope and impact of the vulnerability. Exploit the bug under different scenarios, input variations, user roles, or environmental conditions to ensure that the vulnerability is not limited to specific circumstances. This helps establish the vulnerability's true impact and increases the likelihood of it being accepted and rewarded by the bug bounty program.

Reporting and Communication: Once the bug has been successfully exploited and validated, it is time to report the findings to the bug bounty program owners. Prepare a detailed and well-structured bug report that includes a step-by-step description of the vulnerability, its impact, the steps to reproduce, and the captured evidence. Communicate with the program owners through the designated channels provided by the bug bounty platform or program, adhering to their specified reporting requirements and timelines.

Responsible Disclosure: Throughout the exploitation and validation process, it is crucial to adhere to responsible disclosure practices. Respect the program owners' guidelines regarding disclosure timelines, confidentiality requirements, and any coordinated disclosure processes. Maintain ethical conduct by refraining from unauthorized actions or disclosing sensitive information beyond what is necessary to demonstrate the vulnerability.

By following these steps and ensuring responsible and ethical behavior, bug bounty hunters can effectively exploit and validate discovered bugs. This process provides program owners with the necessary evidence to acknowledge and address the reported vulnerabilities, leading to appropriate fixes and enhancements in the target system's security.

Chapter 4: Building a Bug Bounty Mindset

Welcome to Chapter 4 of "Bug Bounty Success: How to Become a Top Earner in the Bug Bounty Community." In this chapter, we will delve into the importance of building a bug bounty mindset and cultivating the attributes necessary for success in the world of ethical hacking.

Bug hunting requires more than just technical skills. It demands a unique mindset, one that combines curiosity, persistence, and a hunger for continuous improvement. In this chapter, we will explore the key elements of a bug bounty mindset and how they contribute to your effectiveness as a bug bounty hunter.

We'll begin by diving into the development of a hacker mindset. You'll learn to think like an attacker, analyzing systems from a different perspective and anticipating potential vulnerabilities. We'll explore the importance of thinking creatively, being resourceful, and embracing unconventional approaches to uncover hidden security flaws.

Persistence and resilience are crucial qualities in the bug bounty community. We'll discuss the challenges and setbacks you may encounter during your bug hunting journey and how to overcome them. You'll gain strategies for maintaining motivation, pushing through frustration, and learning from failures to become a more resilient bug bounty hunter.

Continuous learning and improvement are cornerstones of success in bug bounties. We'll explore the importance of staying updated with the latest security trends, tools, and techniques. You'll discover resources and strategies for expanding your knowledge, such as participating in online communities, attending conferences, and engaging in hands-on learning experiences.

In addition, we'll discuss the significance of effective time management and organization. Bug hunting requires a structured approach to maximize your productivity and efficiency. You'll learn techniques for prioritizing targets, managing your workflow, and leveraging automation to streamline your bug hunting process.

Throughout this chapter, we'll provide practical tips, exercises, and real-life examples to help you cultivate a bug bounty mindset. You'll gain insights into the mindset of successful bug bounty hunters and how they approach challenges, think outside the box, and continuously improve their skills.

By the end of this chapter, you'll be equipped with the mindset and attributes necessary for bug bounty success. Your hacker mindset, persistence, continuous learning, and effective time management will set you apart and propel you towards becoming a top earner in the bug bounty community.

Prepare yourself to develop the mindset of a successful bug bounty hunter as we continue our journey towards bug bounty success. In the following chapters, we'll explore maximizing your bug bounty earnings, effectively navigating bug bounty platforms, and managing relationships with organizations. Let's dive deeper into the world of ethical hacking and unleash your full potential as a bug bounty hunter.

4.1 Developing a Hacker Mindset

Developing a hacker mindset is crucial for bug bounty hunters to effectively identify vulnerabilities and exploit them ethically. A hacker mindset involves adopting a curious, creative, and relentless approach to uncovering security weaknesses. In this section, we will explore key elements of developing a hacker mindset in bug bounty hunting.

Curiosity and Inquisitiveness: Cultivate a deep curiosity and inquisitive nature to explore systems, applications, and technologies. Develop a desire to understand how things work, identify potential vulnerabilities, and uncover hidden weaknesses. Embrace a mindset of continuous learning, staying up-to-date with the latest security trends, attack techniques, and defensive measures.

Problem-Solving Skills: Develop strong problem-solving skills to think critically and analytically. Bug bounty hunting often requires identifying patterns, connecting the dots, and finding innovative solutions to complex security challenges. Adopt a systematic and logical approach to dissecting applications, networks, and protocols to identify potential attack vectors and vulnerabilities.

Persistence and Perseverance: Bug bounty hunting can be challenging, and success often requires persistence and perseverance. Develop a mindset that embraces setbacks as learning opportunities, remaining resilient in the face of obstacles. Cultivate the determination to dig deeper, try different approaches, and explore alternative angles when faced with roadblocks or initial failures.

Outside-the-Box Thinking: Embrace creative and outside-the-box thinking to uncover vulnerabilities that may not be apparent through conventional methods. Think like an attacker and consider different attack vectors and scenarios. Look beyond the obvious and challenge assumptions to discover novel ways to exploit systems and applications.

Attention to Detail: Pay close attention to detail and adopt a meticulous approach to bug hunting. The ability to spot subtle vulnerabilities, misconfigurations, or anomalies can make a significant difference in uncovering critical weaknesses. Develop a keen eye for identifying patterns, unusual behavior, or inconsistencies that may indicate potential vulnerabilities.

Broad Technical Knowledge: Bug bounty hunters benefit from a broad technical knowledge base encompassing various technologies, frameworks, and protocols. Develop a solid understanding of common web technologies, programming languages, network protocols, and operating systems. This knowledge allows bug bounty hunters to navigate diverse systems, identify vulnerabilities specific to different technologies, and effectively exploit weaknesses.

Ethical Mindset: Maintain an ethical mindset throughout the bug bounty hunting process. Embrace responsible disclosure practices, respect the boundaries set by bug bounty programs, and prioritize the security and privacy of users and organizations. Conduct bug hunting activities with integrity, avoiding malicious actions, and adhering to legal and ethical guidelines.

Continuous Learning and Adaptation: Embrace a mindset of continuous learning and adaptation to stay ahead in the rapidly evolving cybersecurity landscape. Actively seek opportunities to enhance your knowledge and skills through reading, attending conferences, participating in workshops, and engaging with the bug bounty community. Adapt your techniques, tools, and methodologies to keep pace with emerging technologies and evolving attack vectors.

Collaboration and Knowledge Sharing: Embrace a collaborative mindset by actively engaging with the bug bounty community. Participate in forums, discussion groups, and online communities to share knowledge, exchange ideas, and learn from others' experiences. Collaboration fosters growth, expands perspectives, and encourages the development of innovative bug hunting techniques.

Focus on Impact and Value: Prioritize impact and value when selecting targets and reporting vulnerabilities. Concentrate your efforts on identifying vulnerabilities that have a significant impact on security or could be exploited to cause substantial harm. Focus on finding vulnerabilities that provide value to organizations, demonstrating their potential risks and suggesting effective remediation strategies.

By embracing these elements of a hacker mindset, bug bounty hunters can approach their work with a strategic, innovative, and ethical approach. Developing a hacker mindset enhances bug hunters' abilities to identify vulnerabilities, exploit weaknesses, and contribute to the improvement of digital security.

4.2 Persistence and Resilience in Bug Hunting

Persistence and resilience are essential qualities for bug bounty hunters to achieve success in their endeavors. Bug hunting can be a challenging and sometimes frustrating process, requiring determination, perseverance, and the ability to overcome obstacles. In this section, we will explore the importance of persistence and resilience in bug hunting and discuss strategies to cultivate these qualities.

Embrace Setbacks as Learning Opportunities: Bug hunting often involves encountering setbacks and facing challenges. Instead of becoming discouraged, view setbacks as valuable learning opportunities. Analyze the reasons behind failures or rejections and use them to improve your bug hunting techniques and methodologies. Each setback brings valuable insights that can help you become a more effective bug bounty hunter.

Learn from Failures: Failure is an inherent part of the bug hunting journey. Embrace failures as stepping stones to success. Analyze the reasons for failure, whether it's a missed vulnerability or a rejected report, and use those lessons to refine your approach. Learn from your mistakes, adapt your strategies, and continually improve your skills.

Stay Persistent in the Face of Challenges: Bug hunting requires perseverance, as finding vulnerabilities can sometimes be a time-consuming process. Be prepared to invest hours, days, or even weeks in your bug hunting endeavors. Stay committed to your goals, maintain focus, and continue exploring different attack vectors, techniques, and methodologies. Persistence is key to uncovering elusive vulnerabilities that may be hiding in complex systems.

Break Down Complex Problems: When facing a complex target or a challenging vulnerability, break down the problem into smaller, manageable parts. Tackle each component individually, thoroughly exploring different attack vectors and testing various scenarios. Breaking down complex problems helps maintain a sense of progress and prevents overwhelming frustration.

Take Breaks and Maintain Work-Life Balance: Bug hunting can be mentally and physically demanding. It is important to take regular breaks to avoid burnout and maintain a healthy work-life balance. Stepping away from the task at hand and engaging in activities you enjoy can provide a fresh perspective and renewed motivation when you return. Taking care of your well-being ensures sustained focus and effectiveness in your bug hunting efforts.

Seek Support and Collaboration: Engage with the bug bounty community and seek support from fellow bug bounty hunters. Participate in forums, online communities, or local meetups to share experiences, seek advice, and learn from others' insights. Collaboration with like-minded individuals not only fosters a sense of camaraderie but also provides an opportunity to gain new perspectives and approaches to bug hunting.

Celebrate Small Victories: Bug hunting can be a journey of incremental successes. Celebrate and acknowledge each small victory along the way. Whether it's discovering a new vulnerability, successfully exploiting a bug, or receiving recognition for your reports, take the time to appreciate and reward yourself for the progress you make. Celebrating milestones boosts motivation and reinforces the positive aspects of bug hunting.

Stay Updated and Adapt: The field of cybersecurity and bug hunting is constantly evolving. Stay updated with the latest attack techniques, emerging technologies, and new vulnerabilities. Continuously enhance your skills and adapt your strategies to keep pace with changing trends. Embrace a mindset of lifelong learning and remain open to new approaches and methodologies.

Learn from Successful Bug Hunters: Study the approaches and techniques of successful bug hunters in the community. Read their blogs, follow their social media accounts, and study their methodologies. Understand their mindset, problem-solving techniques, and how they overcome challenges. Learn from their experiences and apply those lessons to your own bug hunting journey.

Maintain a Positive Attitude: Cultivate a positive attitude throughout your bug hunting journey. Stay optimistic, even in the face of rejections or prolonged periods without significant findings. A positive mindset helps you maintain focus, stay motivated, and approach challenges with a solution-oriented mindset.

Persistence and resilience are qualities that can be developed over time. By cultivating these qualities, bug bounty hunters can overcome challenges, learn from failures, and achieve greater success in their bug hunting endeavors. Remember that each bug hunt is an opportunity for growth, and maintaining a resilient attitude will ultimately lead to more significant discoveries and contributions to the field of cybersecurity.

4.3 Continuous Learning and Improvement

Continuous learning and improvement are vital for bug bounty hunters to stay ahead in the dynamic field of cybersecurity. The landscape of vulnerabilities, technologies, and attack vectors constantly evolves, requiring bug bounty hunters to continuously update their knowledge, refine their skills, and adapt their strategies. In this section, we will explore the importance of continuous learning and improvement in bug hunting and discuss effective ways to foster growth in this field.

Stay Informed: Keep up-to-date with the latest developments in the cybersecurity industry. Follow reputable sources such as security blogs, news websites, and industry publications to stay informed about emerging vulnerabilities, new attack techniques, and defensive strategies. Engage with the bug bounty community through forums, social media, and conferences to gain insights from fellow bug hunters and industry experts.

Expand Technical Knowledge: Continuously expand your technical knowledge by studying different technologies, programming languages, and protocols. Understand the underlying principles and functionalities of various systems and applications. Stay abreast of the latest advancements in web development, mobile technologies, cloud computing, and network security. This broad knowledge base enables you to effectively identify vulnerabilities across diverse systems.

Learn from Bug Bounty Case Studies: Study real-world bug bounty case studies to gain practical insights into successful vulnerability discoveries and exploitation techniques. Analyze the methodologies, thought processes, and creative approaches employed by other bug hunters. Case studies provide valuable lessons that can be applied to your own bug hunting endeavors.

Engage in Capture the Flag (CTF) Competitions: Participate in Capture the Flag competitions, which simulate real-world hacking scenarios and challenges. CTF competitions offer hands-on experience in identifying and exploiting vulnerabilities across various domains. They allow bug bounty hunters to sharpen their skills, learn new techniques, and collaborate with other participants in a competitive environment.

Practice in Controlled Environments: Set up personal labs or virtual environments to practice different hacking techniques and experiment with various tools. This provides a safe and controlled space to explore vulnerabilities, test exploits, and enhance your practical skills. Practice scenarios that mirror real-world applications and systems to gain valuable experience in finding and exploiting vulnerabilities.

Contribute to Open Source Projects: Contribute to open source projects related to cybersecurity, vulnerability scanning, or penetration testing tools. By contributing to open source projects, you not only give back to the community but also gain hands-on experience, collaborate with experienced developers, and learn from their feedback. It is an excellent opportunity to refine your coding skills and deepen your understanding of security concepts.

Attend Security Conferences and Workshops: Participate in security conferences, workshops, and training programs to learn from industry experts and thought leaders. These events offer opportunities to attend informative talks, hands-on workshops, and networking sessions. Interacting with professionals in the field provides insights into cutting-edge research, emerging threats, and advanced techniques.

Join Bug Bounty Communities: Engage with bug bounty communities and forums to learn from experienced bug hunters, share knowledge, and discuss challenges. Participate in online discussions, ask questions, and contribute to the community by sharing your experiences and insights. Bug bounty communities foster collaboration, provide support, and facilitate ongoing learning opportunities.

Challenge Yourself with New Targets and Technologies: Continuously challenge yourself by targeting different systems, technologies, or industries. Expanding your scope broadens your understanding of various security vulnerabilities and helps you discover new attack vectors. Venture beyond your comfort zone, embrace unfamiliar technologies, and seek opportunities to tackle more complex and diverse bug hunting projects.

Reflect and Analyze: Regularly reflect on your bug hunting experiences, successes, and failures. Analyze your approach, methodologies, and techniques used during each bug hunt. Identify areas for improvement, determine which strategies were effective, and adapt your approach accordingly. This self-analysis helps refine your bug hunting skills, identify areas where additional knowledge is required, and ultimately enhances your overall performance.

By embracing continuous learning and improvement, bug bounty hunters can stay at the forefront of the cybersecurity landscape. Building a solid foundation of technical knowledge, staying informed about emerging threats, and actively seeking opportunities for growth ensures that bug bounty hunters remain effective, adaptable, and successful in their endeavors.

Chapter 5: Maximizing Bug Bounty Earnings

Welcome to Chapter 5 of "Bug Bounty Success: How to Become a Top Earner in the Bug Bounty Community." In this chapter, we will delve into strategies and techniques to help you maximize your bug bounty earnings and increase your success as a bug bounty hunter.

Bug bounties offer not only the thrill of uncovering vulnerabilities but also the opportunity to earn substantial rewards for your efforts. To maximize your earnings, it's essential to approach bug hunting strategically and focus on high-impact targets. In this chapter, we'll explore various strategies to help you optimize your bug bounty journey.

We'll begin by discussing the importance of choosing targets strategically. You'll learn how to identify organizations and applications that offer higher potential for significant vulnerabilities and lucrative rewards. We'll explore factors such as program size, industry, and popularity to guide your target selection process effectively.

Next, we'll dive into exploiting high-impact vulnerabilities. You'll gain insights into vulnerabilities that carry greater weight in terms of severity and potential impact on an organization's security posture.

We'll cover techniques for discovering critical vulnerabilities, such as remote code execution, privilege escalation, and sensitive data exposure, which often result in higher rewards.

Reporting bugs effectively is another crucial aspect of maximizing your earnings. We'll guide you through the process of crafting clear and concise bug reports that effectively communicate the identified vulnerabilities to organizations. You'll learn best practices for providing detailed steps to reproduce, impact analysis, and potential remediation suggestions, enhancing the value of your bug reports.

Additionally, we'll discuss the importance of efficient bug prioritization. With limited time and resources, it's essential to prioritize your bug hunting efforts effectively. You'll gain strategies for assessing the severity, impact, and exploitability of vulnerabilities, allowing you to focus on the most critical issues and maximize your chances of earning rewards.

Throughout this chapter, we'll emphasize the significance of continuous learning and improvement. The bug bounty landscape is constantly evolving, and staying up to date with emerging vulnerabilities, attack techniques, and defensive measures is essential for maximizing your earnings. We'll explore resources and learning strategies to help you stay at the forefront of the field.

By the end of this chapter, you'll have a solid understanding of the strategies and techniques for maximizing your bug bounty earnings. You'll be equipped with the knowledge to choose targets strategically, exploit high-impact vulnerabilities, report bugs effectively, and prioritize your bug hunting efforts for optimal results.

Prepare yourself to elevate your bug bounty earnings as we continue our journey towards bug bounty success. In the following chapters, we'll explore effectively navigating bug bounty platforms, managing relationships with organizations, and advancing your career in the bug bounty community. Let's unlock the secrets to becoming a top earner in the bug bounty community together.

5.1 Choosing Targets Strategically

Choosing targets strategically is a crucial aspect of bug bounty hunting that can significantly impact the success and effectiveness of your bug hunting endeavors. Target selection involves identifying systems, applications, or organizations that have a higher likelihood of containing vulnerabilities and offer greater potential for rewards. In this section, we will explore key considerations and strategies for choosing targets strategically in bug bounty hunting.

Understand Your Expertise and Interests: Start by evaluating your own expertise, skills, and interests. Identify areas of cybersecurity or specific technologies where you have a strong foundation or a genuine passion to learn. Focusing on areas that align with your expertise and interests allows you to leverage your existing knowledge and stay motivated throughout the bug hunting process.

Research Popular Bug Bounty Programs: Conduct research to identify popular bug bounty programs and platforms that attract reputable organizations and offer attractive rewards. Explore platforms such as HackerOne, Bugcrowd, and Synack, which host numerous bug bounty programs. These platforms often provide details about the program's scope, reward structure, and the types of vulnerabilities they are interested in. Prioritize programs that align with your skillset and offer fair rewards.

Assess Target's Reputation and Security Focus: Evaluate the reputation and security focus of the target organization. Look for organizations that prioritize security and have a history of addressing reported vulnerabilities promptly. Research the target's security posture by examining their security announcements, past security incidents, or any public commitments to cybersecurity best practices. Choose targets that demonstrate a genuine commitment to security and are more likely to acknowledge and reward reported vulnerabilities.

Focus on High-Impact Targets: Prioritize targets that have a high impact if a vulnerability is successfully exploited. High-impact targets can include widely used applications, popular websites, critical infrastructure, or systems handling sensitive user data. Exploiting vulnerabilities in high-impact targets not only increases the potential rewards but also contributes to the overall security of a larger user base or organization.

Explore Niche Technologies or Industries: Consider exploring niche technologies, less mainstream applications, or specific industries that may have been overlooked by other bug hunters. Niche technologies or industries often have fewer bug hunters focusing on them, increasing the likelihood of discovering unique vulnerabilities and receiving higher rewards. Niche targets can provide opportunities to showcase your expertise and differentiate yourself in the bug hunting community.

Analyze Bug Bounty Program Scope: Thoroughly analyze the scope of bug bounty programs to understand the targets that are in-scope and eligible for bug hunting. Pay attention to specific exclusions or limitations outlined by the program. Choose programs that align with your expertise, interests, and the types of vulnerabilities you enjoy hunting. Prioritize programs that offer a wide scope or have a focus on the technologies or systems you are particularly skilled in.

Consider Publicly Disclosed Vulnerabilities: Review publicly disclosed vulnerabilities for a target organization or application. Analyze the types of vulnerabilities that have been previously reported and acknowledged. This analysis helps you gauge the potential security weaknesses within the target and identify areas that have received less attention from other bug hunters. By focusing on unexplored areas, you increase your chances of discovering unique vulnerabilities.

Stay Informed about Emerging Technologies: Keep up with emerging technologies and trends in the cybersecurity landscape. Early adoption of new technologies may present opportunities to identify vulnerabilities before they become widely known or effectively mitigated. Stay informed about new frameworks, platforms, or technologies that are gaining popularity, as they often introduce fresh attack vectors and vulnerabilities.

Seek Feedback and Insights from the Bug Bounty Community: Engage with the bug bounty community to gather insights and feedback on potential targets. Participate in bug bounty forums, chat groups, or online communities where bug hunters share their experiences and discuss their target selection strategies. By tapping into the collective wisdom of the community, you can gain valuable perspectives and learn from the experiences of others.

Prioritize Targets Based on Rewards and Recognition: Consider the potential rewards and recognition offered by bug bounty programs when choosing targets. Some bug bounty programs offer higher financial rewards, bonus incentives, or recognition for exceptional findings. Evaluating the potential rewards and recognition can help prioritize targets that provide a better return on investment of your time and effort.

Strategic target selection is crucial for bug bounty hunters to maximize their chances of discovering impactful vulnerabilities and receiving substantial rewards. By considering factors such as expertise, reputation, impact, scope, and emerging technologies, bug bounty hunters can focus their efforts on targets that align with their skills, offer greater potential for success, and contribute to the overall improvement of cybersecurity.

5.2 Exploiting High-Impact Vulnerabilities

Exploiting high-impact vulnerabilities requires a combination of technical skills, careful planning, and a thorough understanding of the target system.

High-impact vulnerabilities often have the potential to cause significant damage, compromise sensitive data, or disrupt critical services. In this section, we will explore key considerations and strategies for effectively exploiting high-impact vulnerabilities in bug bounty hunting.

Understand the Vulnerability: Before attempting to exploit a high-impact vulnerability, ensure that you have a clear understanding of its nature, scope, and potential impact. Analyze the vulnerability's underlying cause, the affected components, and the potential attack vectors. Thoroughly study any available documentation, public disclosures, or proof-of-concept examples to gain insights into the vulnerability's exploitation techniques.

Conduct In-depth Reconnaissance: Perform comprehensive reconnaissance on the target system to gather as much information as possible. Identify potential entry points, exposed services, network infrastructure, or any other elements that can be leveraged for exploitation. Explore the target's attack surface, including web applications, APIs, server configurations, and user interactions, to uncover potential weaknesses.

Develop an Exploitation Plan: Formulate a well-defined plan to exploit the high-impact vulnerability. Consider the potential consequences and collateral damage that the exploitation may cause. Evaluate the feasibility, complexity, and risks associated with different exploitation techniques. A structured plan ensures a systematic and organized approach to the exploitation process.

Verify the Vulnerability: Before proceeding with exploitation, validate the presence and exploitability of the vulnerability. Ensure that the vulnerability is not a false positive or a result of misconfiguration. Perform thorough testing and validation to confirm that the vulnerability can be reliably exploited to achieve the desired impact. Validation helps establish the credibility of your findings and increases the chances of acceptance by the bug bounty program.

Follow Responsible Exploitation Practices: Conduct exploitation activities with utmost responsibility and adherence to ethical guidelines. Avoid causing unnecessary damage or disrupting services during the exploitation process. Limit the scope of your actions to the specific vulnerability being exploited and refrain from accessing or modifying sensitive data beyond what is necessary to demonstrate the impact. Always prioritize the security and privacy of the target system and its users.

Document the Exploitation Process: As you proceed with the exploitation, document each step of the process thoroughly. Capture screenshots, record videos, and log relevant information to provide comprehensive evidence of the exploit. Detailed documentation helps in crafting a clear and concise report and demonstrates the impact of the vulnerability to the bug bounty program owners.

Mitigate Collateral Damage: Take precautions to mitigate any potential collateral damage that may arise during the exploitation process. Implement safeguards to prevent unintended consequences, such as data loss, service disruptions, or unintended access to sensitive information. Consider sandboxed environments, isolated test systems, or controlled conditions to minimize the impact of the exploitation and protect the target and its users.

Exploit Impactfully, Not Destructively: While demonstrating the impact of a high-impact vulnerability, focus on achieving the intended impact without causing unnecessary harm. Emphasize the potential consequences of the vulnerability rather than engaging in destructive actions. Strive to highlight the severity of the vulnerability and its implications without causing permanent damage or compromising the integrity of the target system.

Maintain Effective Communication: Throughout the exploitation process, maintain clear and effective communication with the bug bounty program owners. Regularly update them on your progress, provide them with relevant information and evidence, and seek clarifications if needed. Prompt and transparent communication establishes trust and ensures that the impact and severity of the vulnerability are properly conveyed.

Respect Vulnerability Disclosure Policies: Adhere to the vulnerability disclosure policies set forth by the bug bounty program or platform. Respect any responsible disclosure timelines or coordinated vulnerability disclosure processes specified by the program owners. Abide by any non-disclosure agreements or confidentiality requirements to maintain the integrity of the bug bounty process.

By approaching the exploitation of high-impact vulnerabilities with careful planning, responsible conduct, and effective communication, bug bounty hunters can demonstrate the severity of the vulnerabilities they discover. This helps in ensuring the vulnerabilities are addressed promptly, the target system's security is enhanced, and the bug bounty hunter receives appropriate recognition and rewards for their findings.

5.3 Prioritizing and Reporting Bugs Effectively

Prioritizing and reporting bugs effectively is crucial in bug bounty hunting as it ensures that the discovered vulnerabilities are communicated clearly to the program owners and addressed in a timely manner.

Prioritization helps focus efforts on the most critical vulnerabilities, while effective reporting provides comprehensive information and evidence for the program owners to understand and validate the reported issues. In this section, we will explore strategies for prioritizing and reporting bugs effectively in bug bounty hunting.

Assess the Impact: Evaluate the impact of each discovered vulnerability based on its potential consequences. Consider factors such as the severity of the vulnerability, the potential harm it can cause, and the level of access or control it provides to an attacker. Categorize vulnerabilities into high, medium, and low impact based on their potential impact on the target system's security.

Evaluate the Exploitability: Assess the ease of exploiting each vulnerability. Consider factors such as the level of complexity, required prerequisites, and the likelihood of successful exploitation. Identify vulnerabilities that can be easily and reliably exploited and prioritize them accordingly. Program owners are often more interested in vulnerabilities that have a higher likelihood of being exploited.

Consider the Attack Surface: Analyze the attack surface of the target system and the affected components. Assess the potential impact of vulnerabilities on critical components, sensitive data, or functionality that may be attractive to attackers.

Prioritize vulnerabilities that impact essential system components, expose sensitive data, or allow unauthorized access to critical functionality.

Validate Findings: Before reporting a vulnerability, validate and verify its existence and impact thoroughly. Reproduce the vulnerability in a controlled environment, collect evidence, and document the steps taken to reproduce it. Validate the vulnerability on the latest version of the target system to ensure it has not been patched or mitigated.

Provide Clear and Concise Reports: Craft clear and concise bug reports that effectively communicate the discovered vulnerabilities. Include a detailed description of the vulnerability, including its impact, attack vectors, and any potential mitigations or remediation suggestions. Structure the report in a logical and organized manner, ensuring that the information is easy to understand and follow.

Include Proof of Concept (PoC): Provide a Proof of Concept (PoC) to demonstrate the vulnerability. A PoC serves as tangible evidence and helps program owners understand the vulnerability's impact. Develop a reliable and concise PoC that highlights the steps to reproduce the vulnerability and showcases its potential consequences. Ensure that the PoC is well-documented and can be easily executed by the program owners.

Include Supporting Evidence: Include supporting evidence such as screenshots, videos, or logs that provide additional context and substantiate the reported vulnerability. Capture clear and relevant evidence that showcases the vulnerability in action or the impact it has on the target system. This evidence strengthens the credibility of the report and helps program owners understand the severity of the vulnerability.

Provide Remediation Suggestions: Offer suggestions for mitigating or fixing the vulnerability in your report. Provide clear and actionable recommendations that can help program owners address the vulnerability effectively. Include details on possible mitigations, patches, or best practices that can be implemented to mitigate the risk associated with the vulnerability.

Follow Reporting Guidelines: Adhere to the bug bounty program's reporting guidelines and requirements. Ensure that you report vulnerabilities through the designated channels and follow the program's specified reporting format and timelines. Failure to comply with reporting guidelines may delay the validation and remediation process or even result in the rejection of your report.

Maintain Professionalism and Collaboration: Maintain a professional and respectful attitude when communicating with the program owners. Be responsive to their inquiries, provide clarifications promptly, and engage in a constructive dialogue if needed. Collaboration and effective communication help build a strong rapport with the program owners, increasing the chances of your report being acknowledged and rewarded.

By prioritizing vulnerabilities based on impact and exploitability and reporting them effectively with clear and comprehensive information, bug bounty hunters can ensure that their findings are properly understood and addressed. Effective reporting increases the likelihood of receiving recognition and rewards for your efforts, while also contributing to the improvement of the target system's security.

Chapter 6: Navigating Bug Bounty Platforms

Welcome to Chapter 6 of "Bug Bounty Success: How to Become a Top Earner in the Bug Bounty Community." In this chapter, we will explore the intricacies of bug bounty platforms and provide you with the knowledge and strategies to navigate them effectively.

Bug bounty platforms serve as gateways to numerous bug bounty programs, connecting researchers like you with organizations seeking to enhance their cybersecurity. Understanding the features, rewards, and dynamics of these platforms is crucial for maximizing your bug bounty success. In this chapter, we'll guide you through the process of navigating bug bounty platforms like a pro.

We'll begin by examining the features offered by different bug bounty platforms. Each platform has its unique set of tools, reporting mechanisms, and communication channels. We'll explore common platform features such as vulnerability submission forms, program scopes, and researcher dashboards. Understanding these features will enable you to navigate the platforms efficiently and make the most of the available resources.

Next, we'll dive into the intricacies of bug bounty rewards. Different platforms have varying reward structures and methodologies for determining the value of vulnerabilities. We'll discuss different reward models, such as a flat fee, tiered rewards, or bonuses for critical vulnerabilities. You'll gain insights into how to evaluate the potential financial returns of participating in different bug bounty programs.

Effective automation and tooling are essential for bug bounty success. We'll explore the automation capabilities provided by bug bounty platforms and demonstrate how to leverage them to streamline your bug hunting process. From vulnerability scanners to notification systems, we'll guide you through the tools that can enhance your efficiency and productivity as a bug bounty hunter.

Additionally, we'll discuss the importance of engaging with other researchers and the bug bounty community on these platforms. Collaboration and knowledge sharing can significantly benefit your bug hunting efforts. We'll explore features such as researcher forums, discussion boards, and collaboration opportunities, helping you make the most of the community aspect of bug bounty platforms.

Throughout this chapter, we'll emphasize the significance of understanding the rules, guidelines, and policies set by bug bounty platforms. Each platform has its unique rules of engagement, responsible disclosure requirements, and vulnerability submission guidelines. By familiarizing yourself with these policies, you can ensure a smooth and professional interaction with the platform and the organizations it represents.

By the end of this chapter, you'll be equipped with the knowledge and strategies to navigate bug bounty platforms effectively. You'll understand the platform features, rewards structures, automation tools, and community engagement opportunities available to you. This knowledge will empower you to make informed decisions, select the most suitable programs, and optimize your bug hunting efforts.

Prepare yourself to navigate bug bounty platforms like a seasoned professional as we continue our journey towards bug bounty success. In the following chapters, we'll explore managing relationships with organizations, advancing your career in the bug bounty community, and the ethical and legal considerations of bug bounties. Let's master the art of bug hunting together.

6.1 Understanding Platform Features and Rewards

Understanding the features and rewards offered by bug bounty platforms is essential for bug bounty hunters to maximize their earning potential and effectively navigate the bug bounty ecosystem. Each platform has its own unique set of features, reward structures, and program guidelines. In this section, we will explore key aspects of bug bounty platforms that bug bounty hunters should understand.

Program Scope: Familiarize yourself with the scope of the bug bounty program hosted on the platform. Understand the specific targets, applications, or systems that are eligible for bug hunting. Review the program's rules and guidelines to ensure your bug hunting efforts align with the program's requirements and limitations.

Reward Structure: Gain a thorough understanding of the reward structure of the bug bounty program. Different platforms and programs may offer varied reward models, such as flat bounties, tiered rewards based on vulnerability severity, or bonuses for critical vulnerabilities. Be aware of the potential monetary compensation or other forms of rewards that are offered for successfully reported vulnerabilities.

Vulnerability Severity Levels: Bug bounty platforms often categorize vulnerabilities into different severity levels. These severity levels may include critical, high, medium, and low, or they may follow a different classification system. Understand how the severity levels are defined by the platform and the corresponding rewards associated with each level.

Prioritize your bug hunting efforts on high-severity vulnerabilities to maximize your earning potential.

Program Guidelines and Rules: Familiarize yourself with the guidelines and rules set by the bug bounty platform and the specific program you are targeting. Understand the reporting requirements, disclosure timelines, and any exclusions or limitations mentioned in the program guidelines. Adhering to these guidelines ensures a smooth bug hunting experience and increases your chances of receiving rewards for your findings.

Disclosure Policies: Bug bounty platforms often have specific disclosure policies in place to protect both the program owners and the bug bounty hunters. These policies may include responsible disclosure timelines, coordinated disclosure processes, or non-disclosure agreements (NDAs). Understand and respect these policies to ensure that you handle vulnerabilities and their disclosure in a responsible and ethical manner.

Bug Bounty Platform Features: Explore the features provided by the bug bounty platform. These features may include collaboration tools, discussion forums, bug report templates, vulnerability tracking, and program analytics. Familiarize yourself with these features to leverage them effectively in your bug hunting efforts and to engage with the platform community for support and knowledge sharing.

Reputation and Trustworthiness: Consider the reputation and trustworthiness of the bug bounty platform before participating in bug hunting programs hosted on it. Research the platform's history, user reviews, and the organizations that have engaged with the platform. Choosing reputable and trustworthy bug bounty platforms ensures that your efforts are recognized, and you receive fair treatment for your findings.

Additional Opportunities: Some bug bounty platforms may offer additional opportunities beyond traditional bug hunting programs. These opportunities may include ongoing vulnerability research programs, private bug bounty programs, or special events. Stay updated with these additional opportunities to expand your bug hunting options and increase your earning potential.

Bug Bounty Community Support: Bug bounty platforms often have an active community of bug hunters who share knowledge, provide support, and discuss bug hunting strategies. Engage with the platform community through forums, chat groups, or social media channels. Participating in the community not only helps you stay updated but also provides opportunities for collaboration and learning from experienced bug hunters.

Platform-Specific Tools and Integrations: Some bug bounty platforms offer their own tools, integrations, or API access to facilitate bug hunting. Explore these platform-specific resources and leverage them to streamline your bug hunting workflow, automate certain tasks, or enhance your testing capabilities. These tools and integrations can enhance your productivity and efficiency as a bug bounty hunter.

By understanding the features, rewards, guidelines, and community support provided by bug bounty platforms, bug bounty hunters can effectively navigate the bug bounty ecosystem. This understanding helps bug hunters maximize their earning potential, stay informed about program requirements, and engage with the bug bounty community for support and collaboration.

6.2 Leveraging Automation and Tools

Leveraging automation and tools is a key strategy for bug bounty hunters to enhance their efficiency, scalability, and effectiveness in discovering vulnerabilities. Automation and tools help streamline various tasks, provide deeper analysis, and increase the chances of finding impactful vulnerabilities. In this section, we will explore how bug bounty hunters can effectively leverage automation and tools in their bug hunting endeavors.

Reconnaissance Tools: Use automated reconnaissance tools to gather information about the target system, such as subdomain enumeration, DNS analysis, port scanning, and fingerprinting. Tools like Nmap, Recon-ng, or Shodan can help uncover potential attack vectors and provide a broader understanding of the target's infrastructure.

Scanning and Vulnerability Assessment Tools: Employ scanning tools to automate the process of identifying common vulnerabilities, misconfigurations, or weak points in web applications or networks. Tools like Burp Suite, Nessus, or OpenVAS can assist in automated vulnerability scanning and provide a comprehensive assessment of potential security weaknesses.

Fuzzing Tools: Fuzzing tools automate the process of injecting malformed or unexpected input into an application to discover vulnerabilities. These tools systematically test an application's input fields or APIs for potential buffer overflows, input validation flaws, or other vulnerabilities. Popular fuzzing tools include AFL, OWASP ZAP, and Peach Fuzzer.

Exploitation Frameworks: Utilize exploitation frameworks to streamline the process of exploiting vulnerabilities and validating their impact. Frameworks like Metasploit, BeEF (Browser Exploitation Framework), or ExploitDB provide a comprehensive set of pre-built exploits and payloads that can be customized and used to validate the presence and impact of vulnerabilities.

Web Application Scanners: Employ web application scanners to automatically identify common vulnerabilities in web applications, such as SQL injection, cross-site scripting (XSS), or insecure direct object references. Tools like OWASP ZAP, Nikto, or Acunetix can help detect vulnerabilities by automatically crawling the target application and performing in-depth analysis.

Code Analysis Tools: Leverage code analysis tools to identify potential security vulnerabilities in source code or binary files. These tools can help detect issues like insecure coding practices, input validation flaws, or insecure cryptographic implementations. Popular code analysis tools include SonarQube, FindBugs, and Brakeman.

Collaborative Bug Bounty Platforms: Use collaborative bug bounty platforms that provide features like integrated issue tracking, discussion forums, and collaboration with other bug hunters. These platforms facilitate effective communication with program owners, enable collaboration within the bug bounty community, and streamline the bug reporting process. Examples of such platforms include HackerOne, Bugcrowd, and Synack.

Security Information and Event Management (SIEM) Tools: Integrate SIEM tools into your bug hunting workflow to analyze logs, detect anomalies, and monitor the target system for potential security issues. SIEM tools like Splunk, ELK Stack (Elasticsearch, Logstash, Kibana), or QRadar provide powerful log analysis capabilities that can aid in identifying unusual behavior or potential vulnerabilities.

Automation Scripts: Develop custom automation scripts to perform repetitive tasks, such as scanning, data analysis, or parsing results. These scripts can save time, increase efficiency, and allow for more comprehensive coverage of the target system. Automation scripts can be written in languages like Python, Ruby, or PowerShell, depending on your preferred scripting language.

Continuous Monitoring and Alerting Tools: Employ continuous monitoring and alerting tools to receive notifications about new vulnerabilities, security patches, or emerging threats related to the target system or technologies. Tools like CVE feeds, security blogs, or vulnerability management platforms help you stay updated and proactively identify potential vulnerabilities to target.

While leveraging automation and tools can significantly enhance bug bounty hunting, it's important to maintain a balance and avoid relying solely on automated solutions. Manual testing, creative thinking, and deep analysis are still crucial elements of successful bug hunting. By combining the power of automation and tools with human intuition and expertise, bug bounty hunters can increase their efficiency, uncover impactful vulnerabilities, and contribute to the improvement of cybersecurity.

6.3 Interacting with Other Researchers and the Community

Interacting with other researchers and the bug bounty community is a valuable aspect of bug bounty hunting. Engaging with fellow researchers, sharing knowledge, and collaborating with the community can enhance your skills, provide valuable insights, and foster a supportive environment. In this section, we will explore the benefits of interacting with other researchers and provide strategies for effective community engagement.

Knowledge Sharing: Interacting with other researchers allows you to exchange knowledge, insights, and experiences. Participate in bug bounty forums, online communities, or social media groups dedicated to bug hunting. Share your own findings, ask questions, and contribute to discussions. Actively engaging in knowledge sharing helps expand your understanding of different attack techniques, vulnerability types, and the latest trends in bug hunting.

Collaboration: Collaboration with other researchers can amplify your bug hunting efforts. Form or join bug hunting teams or communities where researchers collaborate on bug hunting projects. Collaborative efforts allow for collective brainstorming, knowledge pooling, and complementary skill sets. Working together increases the chances of discovering vulnerabilities, provides a fresh perspective, and helps in validating findings.

Feedback and Mentorship: Seek feedback and guidance from more experienced bug hunters. Engage with experienced researchers and request their input on your findings, methodologies, or approaches. Their feedback can help refine your bug hunting techniques, improve your reporting skills, and identify areas for growth. Mentorship from experienced bug hunters can be immensely valuable in accelerating your learning and professional development.

Bug Bounty Events and Conferences: Attend bug bounty events, conferences, or meetups to network with fellow researchers, industry professionals, and program owners. These events provide opportunities to interact with experts in the field, learn from their experiences, and establish connections. Engaging in face-to-face interactions allows for deeper discussions, knowledge exchange, and potential collaborations.

Follow Bug Bounty Hunters and Experts: Follow renowned bug bounty hunters, security researchers, and industry experts on social media platforms, blogs, or podcasts. Stay updated with their work, insights, and experiences. Their content often highlights new attack techniques, vulnerability research, and bug hunting strategies. Following these experts keeps you informed about the latest trends and advancements in bug bounty hunting.

Contribute to the Community: Actively contribute to the bug bounty community by sharing your own findings, insights, or research. Publish write-ups, articles, or blog posts that detail your bug hunting experiences, methodologies, and discoveries. Contributing to the community not only helps build your reputation but also provides valuable resources for other bug hunters to learn from.

Ethical and Responsible Conduct: When interacting with other researchers or the bug bounty community, maintain a professional and ethical approach. Respect the work and privacy of fellow researchers, avoid disclosing sensitive information without proper authorization, and adhere to responsible disclosure practices. Foster a supportive and inclusive environment that encourages collaboration, constructive feedback, and ethical bug hunting practices.

Help and Support: Offer assistance and support to other bug hunters, particularly newcomers to the field. Share your knowledge, provide guidance, and answer questions. A supportive community encourages growth, collaboration, and the overall advancement of bug hunting as a profession.

Engage with Program Owners: Interact with bug bounty program owners in a professional and respectful manner. Maintain clear and prompt communication, address any clarifications they may have, and provide comprehensive reports for your findings. Building a good rapport with program owners increases the likelihood of your reports being acknowledged, validated, and rewarded.

Stay Positive and Encourage Others: Maintain a positive attitude and encourage others in the bug bounty community. Celebrate their successes, provide words of encouragement, and offer support during challenging times. A positive and supportive community fosters a collaborative and inclusive environment where bug hunters can thrive.

Interacting with other researchers and engaging with the bug bounty community enriches your bug hunting journey. The collective knowledge, experiences, and support of the community can significantly enhance your skills, expand your network, and contribute to your overall success as a bug bounty hunter.

Chapter 7: Managing Relationships with Organizations

Welcome to Chapter 7 of "Bug Bounty Success: How to Become a Top Earner in the Bug Bounty Community." In this chapter, we will explore the importance of building and maintaining positive relationships with organizations as a bug bounty hunter.

As a bug bounty hunter, your interactions with organizations are crucial to your success. Developing strong relationships with organizations not only enhances your bug hunting experience but also paves the way for long-term partnerships and increased earning potential. In this chapter, we'll delve into strategies for managing relationships with organizations effectively.

We'll begin by discussing the establishment of professional communication channels. Clear and effective communication is essential for a smooth bug hunting experience. We'll explore best practices for interacting with organizations, including methods of contact, response expectations, and maintaining a professional tone. You'll learn how to present yourself as a trusted and reliable bug bounty hunter.

Responsible disclosure is a fundamental aspect of bug hunting. We'll delve into the proper procedures for reporting vulnerabilities to organizations ethically and responsibly. You'll gain insights into the importance of providing clear and concise bug reports, including relevant technical details and steps to reproduce the vulnerability. We'll also explore the significance of respecting organizations' disclosure preferences and guidelines.

Building long-term partnerships can be highly beneficial for bug bounty hunters. We'll discuss strategies for fostering relationships with organizations beyond individual bug reports. You'll learn how to provide value beyond bug hunting, such as offering security recommendations or assisting with security testing initiatives. Cultivating these relationships can lead to repeat engagements, increased rewards, and additional opportunities for collaboration.

We'll also explore the dynamics of bug triage and validation processes within organizations. Understanding how organizations handle and prioritize reported vulnerabilities is crucial for managing expectations and maintaining effective communication. We'll discuss common bug triage practices and provide insights into how to navigate these processes professionally.

Throughout this chapter, we'll emphasize the importance of professionalism, integrity, and ethical conduct when dealing with organizations. Upholding ethical standards and treating organizations with respect and transparency will not only enhance your reputation as a bug bounty hunter but also strengthen your relationships with organizations in the long run.

By the end of this chapter, you'll have the knowledge and strategies to manage relationships with organizations effectively. You'll understand how to establish professional communication channels, engage in responsible disclosure, foster long-term partnerships, and navigate bug triage and validation processes. These skills will position you as a trusted and respected bug bounty hunter, paving the way for continued success in the bug bounty community.

Prepare yourself to cultivate strong relationships with organizations as we continue our journey towards bug bounty success. In the following chapters, we'll explore bug bounty case studies, advancing your career in the bug bounty community, and the ethical and legal considerations of bug bounties. Let's forge meaningful connections and excel in the art of bug hunting together.

7.1 Establishing Professional Communication Channels

Establishing professional communication channels is essential for bug bounty hunters to effectively communicate with bug bounty program owners, fellow researchers, and other relevant stakeholders. Professional communication channels ensure clear and efficient information exchange, facilitate collaboration, and maintain a positive reputation in the bug bounty community. In this section, we will explore strategies for establishing professional communication channels in bug bounty hunting.

Email Communication: Email is a common and widely accepted communication method in bug bounty hunting. Use a professional email address that reflects your identity or bug hunting brand. When communicating via email, be concise, clear, and professional in your language. Clearly mention the purpose of your email, provide relevant details, and address the recipient respectfully. Respond to emails promptly to maintain effective communication.

Bug Bounty Platforms: Bug bounty platforms often provide dedicated communication channels between bug bounty hunters and program owners. Utilize these platforms to report vulnerabilities, seek clarifications, or provide additional information. Follow the platform's guidelines for communication, including using the designated messaging features or comment threads for efficient and organized discussions.

Chat and Collaboration Tools: Leverage chat and collaboration tools for real-time communication with other researchers or team members. Platforms like Slack, Discord, or Microsoft Teams offer features such as group discussions, direct messaging, and file sharing. Join relevant bug bounty community channels or create your own channels for focused discussions and collaboration.

Public Bug Bounty Forums: Participate in public bug bounty forums and discussion boards to engage with the bug bounty community. Platforms like Bugcrowd Forum, HackerOne Community, or Reddit's r/netsec provide opportunities to ask questions, seek advice, and share insights. Follow the forum guidelines, be respectful, and contribute constructively to maintain a positive and professional presence.

Social Media Presence: Maintain a professional presence on social media platforms such as Twitter or LinkedIn. Connect with fellow bug bounty hunters, program owners, and industry professionals. Use social media to share bug hunting experiences, research findings, or relevant news. Engage in professional conversations, offer insights, and foster positive interactions within the bug bounty community.

Web Presence and Personal Blog: Establish a web presence or maintain a personal blog to showcase your bug hunting journey, research findings, or write-ups. This provides a platform for others to learn about your expertise, and it serves as a professional portfolio. Include contact information and encourage visitors to reach out to you through appropriate channels for bug hunting-related discussions or collaborations.

Professional Networking Events: Attend bug bounty events, conferences, or local meetups to network with program owners, fellow researchers, and industry professionals. These events offer opportunities for face-to-face interactions, which can lead to more in-depth discussions and collaborations. Exchange contact information and follow up with relevant individuals after the event to continue professional communication.

Language and Tone: Maintain a professional tone and language in all your communications. Be polite, respectful, and considerate in your interactions. Avoid using offensive or aggressive language, even when faced with disagreements or challenges. Clear and concise communication helps avoid misunderstandings and promotes effective collaboration.

Confidentiality and Non-Disclosure Agreements: Respect any confidentiality or non-disclosure agreements (NDAs) you enter into with program owners. Safeguard sensitive information, avoid discussing vulnerabilities outside of authorized channels, and adhere to the agreed-upon disclosure timelines. Maintaining confidentiality demonstrates professionalism and establishes trust with program owners.

Timely and Responsive Communication: Be prompt and responsive in your communication with bug bounty program owners, fellow researchers, or other stakeholders. Respond to inquiries, requests for clarification, or feedback in a timely manner. Keeping the lines of communication open and maintaining regular engagement establishes your reliability and professionalism.

Establishing professional communication channels in bug bounty hunting is crucial for successful collaboration, effective bug reporting, and maintaining a positive reputation. Clear and respectful communication enhances your relationships within the bug bounty community, strengthens your network, and increases your chances of receiving recognition for your findings.

7.2 Reporting Vulnerabilities Responsibly

Reporting vulnerabilities responsibly is a critical aspect of bug bounty hunting. It ensures that the discovered vulnerabilities are communicated in a manner that prioritizes the security of the affected systems and users, maintains a professional approach, and fosters a positive relationship with bug bounty program owners. In this section, we will explore strategies for responsibly reporting vulnerabilities in bug bounty hunting.

Understand Responsible Disclosure: Familiarize yourself with the concept of responsible disclosure and the associated guidelines. Responsible disclosure emphasizes reporting vulnerabilities directly to the program owners or relevant stakeholders first, giving them an opportunity to address and mitigate the vulnerability before making it public. Adhering to responsible disclosure practices demonstrates your commitment to security and responsible bug hunting.

Follow Program Guidelines: Carefully review the bug bounty program's guidelines, rules, and disclosure policies. Each program may have specific instructions on how to report vulnerabilities, disclosure timelines, and any exclusions or limitations. Adhere to these guidelines to ensure that your report is in line with the program's requirements and expectations.

Gather Comprehensive Information: Provide detailed and comprehensive information in your vulnerability report. Include a clear and concise description of the vulnerability, including the affected components, potential impact, and steps to reproduce the issue. Document your findings with screenshots, videos, or any other supporting evidence to help program owners understand and validate the vulnerability.

Respect Confidentiality: Respect the confidentiality of the bug bounty program and any non-disclosure agreements (NDAs) you may have agreed to. Avoid discussing or disclosing vulnerabilities outside of authorized channels or without proper authorization from the program owners. Safeguard sensitive information to prevent unauthorized access or potential harm.

Prioritize Critical Vulnerabilities: When reporting multiple vulnerabilities, prioritize critical vulnerabilities that have a higher potential for significant harm or impact. Focus on vulnerabilities that allow unauthorized access, compromise sensitive data, or have the potential to disrupt critical services. By prioritizing critical vulnerabilities, you enable program owners to address the most severe issues promptly.

Clear and Concise Reporting: Craft your vulnerability report in a clear and concise manner. Clearly explain the steps to reproduce the vulnerability, including the necessary prerequisites or specific configurations. Use screenshots, videos, or other visual aids to demonstrate the vulnerability in action. Avoid unnecessary technical jargon and provide explanations that are easily understandable by both technical and non-technical stakeholders.

Suggest Mitigations or Remediations: Offer suggestions for mitigating or remedying the vulnerability in your report. Provide clear and actionable recommendations that can help program owners address the issue effectively. Share any additional information or resources that can assist in the resolution process, such as code snippets, patches, or best practices.

Timely Reporting: Report vulnerabilities to the bug bounty program owners promptly after their discovery. Timely reporting allows program owners to assess the severity of the vulnerability and initiate the necessary mitigation measures promptly. Follow any specified reporting timelines or coordinated disclosure processes outlined by the program.

Maintain Professionalism and Respect: Maintain a professional and respectful approach when communicating with bug bounty program owners. Be polite, patient, and understanding throughout the entire reporting process. Respond promptly to any inquiries or requests for additional information, and address feedback or questions in a professional manner.

Be Responsive to Program Owners: Be responsive and cooperative when working with program owners. Maintain open lines of communication, provide clarifications if needed, and promptly address any concerns or questions they may have. Demonstrating a collaborative and helpful attitude builds trust and establishes a positive relationship with program owners.

By responsibly reporting vulnerabilities, bug bounty hunters contribute to the overall security of the target systems, establish themselves as trusted professionals, and enhance the bug bounty community's reputation. Responsible disclosure practices prioritize the interests of all stakeholders involved, ensuring that vulnerabilities are handled in a manner that minimizes potential harm and fosters a secure digital ecosystem.

7.3 Building Long-Term Partnerships

Building long-term partnerships is a valuable aspect of bug bounty hunting that can lead to ongoing collaborations, increased opportunities, and a mutually beneficial relationship with bug bounty program owners. Long-term partnerships offer stability, trust, and continuous growth in the bug hunting ecosystem. In this section, we will explore strategies for building long-term partnerships in bug bounty hunting.

Deliver High-Quality Reports: Consistently provide high-quality vulnerability reports that are well-documented, comprehensive, and actionable. Demonstrate your expertise, attention to detail, and thoroughness in your findings. Delivering well-crafted reports showcases your professionalism and establishes a foundation of trust with program owners.

Maintain Professional Communication: Maintain open and professional lines of communication with bug bounty program owners. Respond promptly to their inquiries, provide clarifications when needed, and engage in constructive discussions. Clear and effective communication fosters trust, facilitates collaboration, and strengthens the partnership.

Demonstrate Value: Go beyond just finding vulnerabilities. Provide value to bug bounty program owners by offering insights, suggesting improvements, or helping with remediation efforts. Offer your expertise and guidance on enhancing the security of their systems. By showcasing your value as a trusted advisor, you solidify your position as a valuable long-term partner.

Respect Confidentiality: Respect any confidentiality or non-disclosure agreements (NDAs) established with bug bounty program owners. Safeguard sensitive information, avoid unauthorized disclosures, and handle vulnerabilities with the utmost care.

Respecting confidentiality builds trust and demonstrates your professionalism and commitment to security.

Collaborate on Improvements: Collaborate with program owners to improve their bug bounty programs and security posture. Share your experiences, provide feedback on program guidelines, and offer suggestions for program enhancements. Actively engaging in discussions about program improvements shows your commitment to the program's success and can lead to a deeper and more meaningful partnership.

Participate in Private Bug Bounty Programs: Private bug bounty programs offer an opportunity to work closely with program owners on a long-term basis. Engage in private programs where you can establish a direct relationship with the organization. Private programs often provide higher rewards, exclusive access, and a deeper understanding of the organization's security needs.

Maintain a Positive Reputation: Build and maintain a positive reputation within the bug bounty community. Demonstrate professionalism, ethical conduct, and a helpful attitude towards fellow researchers and program owners. A positive reputation increases your credibility, attracts program owners' attention, and opens doors for long-term partnerships.

Offer Vulnerability Research Services: Consider offering vulnerability research services beyond bug bounty programs. Develop a portfolio of your expertise and offer your services directly to organizations looking to enhance their security. Building a reputation as a reliable and skilled vulnerability researcher can lead to long-term partnerships with organizations seeking ongoing security support.

Continuously Upgrade Your Skills: Stay updated with the latest security trends, attack techniques, and defensive measures. Continuously upgrade your skills through learning, certifications, and participating in relevant training programs. Demonstrating a commitment to professional growth and knowledge ensures that you can provide value to bug bounty program owners in an evolving security landscape.

Foster a Collaborative Mindset: Embrace a collaborative mindset when working with program owners and fellow researchers. Share knowledge, engage in discussions, and support each other's growth. By fostering a collaborative environment, you contribute to the overall success of the bug bounty community and build strong, long-lasting partnerships.

Building long-term partnerships in bug bounty hunting requires consistent dedication, professionalism, and a focus on delivering value. By establishing trust, maintaining open communication, and actively contributing to the security of the organizations you work with, you can cultivate partnerships that extend beyond individual bug bounty programs and create a foundation for continued collaboration and growth.

Chapter 8: Bug Bounty Case Studies

Welcome to Chapter 8 of "Bug Bounty Success: How to Become a Top Earner in the Bug Bounty Community." In this chapter, we will delve into real-life bug bounty case studies, analyzing successful bug reports and drawing valuable lessons from these experiences.

Bug bounty case studies provide valuable insights into the world of bug hunting. By examining real-world examples, we can gain a deeper understanding of the vulnerabilities, techniques, and impact of bug discoveries. In this chapter, we'll explore a range of bug bounty case studies to enhance your bug hunting skills and knowledge.

We'll begin by dissecting successful bug reports. You'll learn how to analyze the structure, content, and technical details of well-crafted reports. We'll explore the components of a comprehensive bug report, including vulnerability description, impact analysis, and proof-of-concept demonstrations. By understanding the elements of an effective bug report, you'll be able to improve the quality and impact of your own reports.

Next, we'll explore various types of vulnerabilities and their impact. We'll dive into case studies showcasing common vulnerabilities such as cross-site scripting (XSS), SQL injection, server-side request forgery (SSRF), and more. You'll gain insights into the severity and consequences of these vulnerabilities, along with the potential risks they pose to organizations.

Through case studies, you'll also learn about the creative approaches and unconventional techniques used by bug bounty hunters to uncover vulnerabilities. We'll delve into innovative bug discoveries, including chained vulnerabilities, logical flaws, and combination attacks. By studying these examples, you'll expand your bug hunting toolkit and discover new avenues for finding critical bugs.

Furthermore, we'll explore the broader impact of bug bounty programs on organizations' security posture. We'll discuss case studies where bug bounty reports led to significant improvements in security practices, code reviews, and overall risk mitigation. Understanding the value and impact of bug bounty programs beyond individual vulnerabilities will help you communicate the importance of your bug reports effectively.

Throughout this chapter, we'll provide analysis, insights, and practical takeaways from each case study. By studying real-life examples, you'll gain a deeper understanding of the bug bounty landscape and refine your bug hunting skills. These case studies will inspire you to think creatively, explore new attack vectors, and approach bug hunting from different angles.

By the end of this chapter, you'll have a rich repertoire of bug bounty case studies to draw inspiration from. You'll understand the structure of successful bug reports, the impact of various vulnerabilities, and the creative techniques employed by bug bounty hunters. Armed with this knowledge, you'll be better equipped to identify, exploit, and report vulnerabilities that make a real impact.

Prepare yourself to dive into the fascinating world of bug bounty case studies as we continue our journey towards bug bounty success. In the following chapters, we'll explore advancing your career in the bug bounty community, the ethical and legal considerations of bug bounties, and the future of bug bounty programs. Let's learn from real-world examples and sharpen our bug hunting skills together.

8.1 Real-Life Success Stories and Lessons Learned

Real-life success stories in bug bounty hunting not only inspire aspiring bug hunters but also provide valuable insights and lessons that can guide their own bug hunting journeys. In this section, we will explore some real-life success stories and the lessons learned from them.

Success Story 1: "The Million Dollar Bug Bounty"

One remarkable success story is that of Santiago Lopez, who became the first bug bounty hunter to reach the milestone of earning $1 million through bug bounty programs. Santiago started bug hunting as a teenager and dedicated himself to honing his skills. He actively participated in various bug bounty platforms, reported numerous vulnerabilities, and received generous rewards. His success story showcases the potential for bug bounty hunters to achieve significant financial success by continuously improving their skills and staying dedicated to their craft.

Lesson Learned: Consistency and Persistence Pay Off

Santiago's success demonstrates the importance of consistency and persistence in bug bounty hunting. He consistently worked on improving his skills, participating in bug bounty programs, and reporting vulnerabilities. By consistently dedicating time and effort to bug hunting, Santiago was able to accumulate a substantial income over time. This highlights the significance of persistent learning, practice, and regular bug hunting engagement to achieve success in the long run.

Success Story 2: "The Critical Infrastructure Discovery"

A bug bounty hunter, who prefers to remain anonymous, discovered a critical vulnerability in a widely used industrial control system. The vulnerability could have potentially allowed unauthorized access and control over critical infrastructure, posing a severe risk to public safety. The bug hunter responsibly reported the vulnerability to the program owner, leading to its prompt remediation. This success story emphasizes the importance of bug hunting in identifying and mitigating vulnerabilities that can have significant real-world consequences.

Lesson Learned: Impactful Discoveries Can Safeguard Society

The lesson from this success story is that bug bounty hunting can have a direct and positive impact on society by identifying vulnerabilities in critical systems. By diligently searching for vulnerabilities, bug hunters play a crucial role in securing essential infrastructure, protecting public safety, and mitigating potential risks. This success story serves as a reminder of the importance of bug hunting in safeguarding the technological foundations that support our daily lives.

Success Story 3: "The Bug Hunter Turned Security Professional"

Another success story involves a bug bounty hunter who gained recognition for their exceptional skills and ethical hacking abilities. Their expertise and reputation as a bug bounty hunter led to opportunities to work as a security professional for reputable organizations. This success story demonstrates how bug bounty hunting can serve as a stepping stone to a successful career in cybersecurity.

Lesson Learned: Bug Hunting Can Open Doors to Professional Opportunities

This success story highlights the potential for bug hunting to open doors to professional opportunities beyond monetary rewards. By showcasing their skills and knowledge through bug hunting, individuals can attract the attention of organizations seeking security professionals. This success story emphasizes the value of bug hunting as a path to a rewarding career in cybersecurity.

In conclusion, real-life success stories in bug bounty hunting provide valuable lessons for aspiring bug hunters. They emphasize the importance of consistency, persistence, and continuous improvement in bug hunting endeavors. These success stories also underscore the significant impact bug hunters can have by identifying critical vulnerabilities and contributing to the security of society. Furthermore, they showcase the potential for bug hunting to lead to professional growth and career opportunities in the field of cybersecurity. By learning from these success stories, bug hunters can gain valuable insights and motivation to excel in their bug hunting journeys.

8.2 Analyzing Vulnerabilities and Their Impact

Analyzing vulnerabilities and their impact is a crucial step in bug bounty hunting. By thoroughly understanding vulnerabilities and their potential consequences, bug bounty hunters can provide accurate and actionable information to program owners, prioritize their bug hunting efforts effectively, and contribute to the overall security of the target systems. In this section, we will explore strategies for analyzing vulnerabilities and assessing their impact.

Vulnerability Identification: Start by identifying and categorizing the vulnerabilities you discover. Classify them based on their nature, such as software flaws, configuration weaknesses, or logical errors. Assign unique identifiers or labels to each vulnerability for easy reference and tracking.

Vulnerability Scoring and Severity Assessment: Assign a severity level to each vulnerability based on industry-standard scoring systems, such as the Common Vulnerability Scoring System (CVSS). Consider factors such as the exploitability, potential impact, and affected assets or data. This scoring helps program owners understand the relative severity and prioritize their remediation efforts.

Impact Assessment: Assess the potential impact of each vulnerability on the target system and its users. Consider the worst-case scenario that could result from the exploitation of the vulnerability. Evaluate the potential consequences in terms of data breaches, unauthorized access, service disruption, financial losses, or reputational damage. This assessment helps prioritize the most critical vulnerabilities for immediate attention.

Attack Surface Analysis: Analyze the attack surface of the target system to determine the potential reach and impact of a vulnerability. Consider the exposed entry points, interfaces, user inputs, and dependencies. Identify vulnerabilities that allow attackers to gain unauthorized access, manipulate data, or compromise critical components within the attack surface.

Chain of Exploitation: Evaluate the potential for chaining vulnerabilities together to escalate privileges or achieve a more significant impact. Determine if a single vulnerability can lead to the exploitation of other vulnerabilities or enable attackers to bypass security measures. Assess the impact of such chains of exploitation on the confidentiality, integrity, and availability of the target system.

Data Sensitivity and Compliance Considerations: Assess the potential impact of vulnerabilities on the confidentiality and integrity of sensitive data. Consider applicable data protection regulations, industry standards, or compliance requirements. Evaluate the impact of vulnerabilities on compliance with regulations like the General Data Protection Regulation (GDPR), Payment Card Industry Data Security Standard (PCI DSS), or Health Insurance Portability and Accountability Act (HIPAA).

Contextual Factors: Consider contextual factors that may influence the impact of a vulnerability. Evaluate the potential impact based on the specific environment, system architecture, user base, or the sensitivity of the data processed. Assess the potential consequences from the perspective of the organization's business operations and the potential harm to its reputation.

Proof of Concept (PoC) Validation: Validate the impact of vulnerabilities by developing or executing Proof of Concept (PoC) scenarios. Create reliable and controlled environments to reproduce and demonstrate the exploitation of the vulnerabilities.

Validate that the vulnerabilities can be exploited successfully and showcase their potential consequences to program owners.

Mitigation and Remediation Recommendations: Provide actionable recommendations for mitigating or remediating the vulnerabilities. Offer suggestions on configuration changes, code fixes, security controls, or best practices that can effectively address the vulnerabilities. Provide clear and concise guidance to program owners on steps they can take to mitigate the risks associated with the vulnerabilities.

Documentation and Reporting: Document your vulnerability analysis findings in a clear and organized manner. Prepare vulnerability reports that provide a comprehensive overview of the vulnerabilities, their impact, and any supporting evidence. Use screenshots, videos, or other visual aids to enhance the clarity of the reports. Ensure that the reports are easy to understand by both technical and non-technical stakeholders.

By thoroughly analyzing vulnerabilities and assessing their impact, bug bounty hunters can effectively communicate the severity and consequences to program owners. This enables program owners to prioritize their remediation efforts, allocate resources efficiently, and improve the security posture of the target systems. A well-rounded vulnerability analysis contributes to the overall success of bug bounty hunting and helps in building a more secure digital landscape.

8.3 Demonstrating Creative Approaches to Bug Hunting

Demonstrating creative approaches to bug hunting is essential for bug bounty hunters to stand out from the crowd and discover vulnerabilities that may go unnoticed through conventional methods. Creative bug hunting techniques can help uncover unique attack vectors, expose complex vulnerabilities, and contribute to the overall improvement of system security. In this section, we will explore strategies for demonstrating creative approaches to bug hunting.

Think Outside the Box: Challenge conventional assumptions and think beyond typical attack vectors. Look for innovative ways to exploit the target system by considering alternative scenarios, edge cases, or unusual user interactions. Avoid restricting yourself to known vulnerabilities or established techniques and explore uncharted territory.

Experiment with Different Input Types: Test the target system with various types of inputs to uncover unexpected behavior. Try different data formats, special characters, or large data payloads to identify potential input validation or parsing vulnerabilities.

Creative input manipulation can lead to the discovery of injection, cross-site scripting (XSS), or other input-related vulnerabilities.

Utilize Fuzzing Techniques: Fuzzing involves feeding a system with unexpected or random inputs to identify vulnerabilities. Experiment with different fuzzing approaches, such as mutation-based fuzzing, generation-based fuzzing, or intelligent fuzzing. Apply fuzzing techniques to various components, such as network protocols, file formats, or user inputs, to uncover unique vulnerabilities.

Combine Multiple Vulnerabilities: Look for opportunities to chain multiple vulnerabilities together to achieve a more significant impact. Exploit one vulnerability to gain access or escalate privileges, and then leverage that access to exploit another vulnerability. Chaining vulnerabilities requires creativity and a deep understanding of the target system's architecture and attack surface.

Reverse Engineering and Code Analysis: Apply reverse engineering techniques to analyze binaries, firmware, or proprietary protocols. Disassemble and analyze the code to uncover vulnerabilities that may be hidden from traditional testing methods. By understanding the inner workings of the target system, you can identify unique attack vectors and potential vulnerabilities.

Explore Lesser-Known Technologies: Investigate less popular or emerging technologies that may have limited bug hunting activity. These technologies often have less scrutiny, making them potential treasure troves for discovering vulnerabilities. Learn about their architecture, specifications, and common pitfalls to identify weaknesses that others may have overlooked.

Focus on Business Logic Flaws: Analyze the target system's business logic to identify flaws that may lead to unexpected or unintended behaviors. Look for logic flaws that could enable unauthorized access, privilege escalation, or bypass of security controls. Creative thinking and an understanding of the system's intended behavior are crucial in identifying such vulnerabilities.

Participate in Capture the Flag (CTF) Competitions: Engage in Capture the Flag competitions, which offer challenges designed to test and improve your hacking skills. CTFs often require a creative and unconventional approach to solve complex puzzles and find hidden vulnerabilities. These competitions provide an excellent opportunity to showcase your creative bug hunting techniques and learn from others in the community.

Collaborate and Share Insights: Engage with the bug bounty community, participate in discussions, and share insights with fellow bug hunters. Collaborative brainstorming sessions and knowledge sharing can inspire new ideas and approaches to bug hunting. By exchanging insights and learning from others, you can enhance your creativity and broaden your bug hunting capabilities.

Document and Share Success Stories: Document your creative bug hunting approaches and success stories. Publish write-ups, blog posts, or whitepapers detailing the vulnerabilities you discovered, the unique techniques you used, and the lessons learned. Sharing your experiences not only contributes to the bug hunting community but also establishes your reputation as a creative and skilled bug hunter.

Demonstrating creative approaches to bug hunting not only helps in discovering vulnerabilities that others may have missed but also establishes your unique skill set and expertise. By thinking outside the box, exploring unconventional attack vectors, and sharing your insights with the community, you contribute to the continuous improvement of system security and elevate the bug hunting field as a whole.

Chapter 9: Bug Bounty Ethics and Legal Considerations

Welcome to Chapter 9 of "Bug Bounty Success: How to Become a Top Earner in the Bug Bounty Community." In this chapter, we will delve into the crucial topic of bug bounty ethics and legal considerations, guiding you on how to navigate the ethical and legal aspects of bug hunting responsibly.

As bug bounty hunters, we have a responsibility to uphold ethical standards, respect legal boundaries, and prioritize the security and privacy of organizations. In this chapter, we'll explore the ethical dilemmas that may arise in bug hunting and provide guidance on responsible disclosure and ethical conduct.

We'll begin by discussing the importance of respecting legal boundaries and guidelines. Bug hunting should always be conducted within the confines of the law. We'll explore the legal considerations surrounding bug bounties, including relevant legislation, terms of service, and bug bounty program rules. By understanding the legal landscape, you can ensure that your bug hunting activities are conducted lawfully and ethically.

Responsible disclosure is a critical aspect of bug hunting. We'll delve into the principles of responsible disclosure, emphasizing the importance of communicating vulnerabilities to organizations in a responsible and transparent manner. You'll learn about coordinated disclosure processes, appropriate timeframes for disclosure, and best practices for working with organizations to address vulnerabilities.

Ethical dilemmas may arise in bug hunting, and it's essential to approach them with integrity and ethical decision-making. We'll explore scenarios where ethical considerations may come into play, such as discovering sensitive data, accessing unauthorized systems, or unintentionally causing disruption. You'll gain insights into how to navigate these situations ethically and responsibly.

Furthermore, we'll discuss the importance of bug bounty community engagement and fostering a positive and collaborative environment. Sharing knowledge, mentoring newcomers, and contributing to the bug bounty community are essential aspects of ethical bug hunting. We'll explore ways to actively participate in the community, contribute to open-source projects, and promote responsible bug hunting practices.

Throughout this chapter, we'll emphasize the significance of transparency, honesty, and integrity in bug hunting. Upholding ethical standards not only ensures a positive reputation for yourself but also contributes to the overall trustworthiness of the bug bounty community. By conducting yourself ethically and responsibly, you can help shape the future of bug bounty programs.

By the end of this chapter, you'll have a solid understanding of bug bounty ethics and legal considerations. You'll be equipped with the knowledge to navigate the legal landscape, engage in responsible disclosure, address ethical dilemmas, and actively contribute to the bug bounty community in an ethical and transparent manner.

Prepare yourself to approach bug hunting with integrity and ethical decision-making as we continue our journey towards bug bounty success. In the following chapters, we'll explore advancing your career in the bug bounty community, the future of bug bounties, and the continuous learning and adaptability required for long-term success. Let's be ethical and responsible bug bounty hunters together.

9.1 Respecting Legal Boundaries and Guidelines

Respecting legal boundaries and guidelines is of utmost importance in bug bounty hunting. Bug hunters must operate within the confines of the law, adhere to ethical standards, and follow the guidelines set by bug bounty platforms and program owners.

Respecting legal boundaries ensures responsible and ethical bug hunting practices, protects the interests of all stakeholders involved, and helps maintain the integrity of the bug bounty community. In this section, we will explore strategies for respecting legal boundaries and guidelines in bug bounty hunting.

Familiarize Yourself with Laws and Regulations: Understand the legal landscape and relevant laws related to bug bounty hunting in your jurisdiction. Familiarize yourself with laws such as the Computer Fraud and Abuse Act (CFAA) in the United States or similar legislation in your country. Stay updated with any changes or updates to legal frameworks to ensure your bug hunting activities comply with the law.

Obtain Proper Authorization: Only engage in bug hunting activities on systems or platforms for which you have explicit authorization. Participate in bug bounty programs that clearly state the scope and rules of engagement. Do not attempt to access systems or applications without proper authorization, as unauthorized access can lead to legal consequences.

Respect Scope Limitations: Respect the defined scope of the bug bounty program or project. Do not test systems, networks, or applications that are explicitly out of scope. Stay within the designated boundaries set by the program owners and focus your bug hunting efforts on the specified targets.

Follow Bug Bounty Platform Guidelines: Adhere to the guidelines provided by bug bounty platforms where you participate. Each platform has its own set of rules, policies, and disclosure guidelines. Familiarize yourself with these guidelines and ensure that your bug hunting activities align with the platform's requirements. Failure to follow platform guidelines can lead to account suspension or removal from the platform.

Responsible Disclosure: Practice responsible disclosure when reporting vulnerabilities. Respect the disclosure timelines set by the program owners and follow their preferred communication channels. Avoid publicly disclosing vulnerabilities before the program owners have had a reasonable opportunity to remediate them. Responsible disclosure helps protect users, gives program owners the chance to address vulnerabilities, and maintains a cooperative relationship with the organization.

Obtain Consent for Testing: Obtain explicit consent from program owners or system administrators before performing any testing or vulnerability assessment activities. Seek permission before conducting any security tests, such as scanning, probing, or exploiting vulnerabilities. Unauthorized testing can be perceived as an attack and can lead to legal repercussions.

Protect User Privacy and Data: Respect user privacy and handle any sensitive data you encounter responsibly. Avoid accessing, collecting, or tampering with personal or sensitive information during your bug hunting activities. If you encounter personal data inadvertently, handle it in accordance with applicable data protection laws and immediately report it to the program owners.

Non-Disclosure Agreements (NDAs): Honor any non-disclosure agreements (NDAs) you enter into with program owners or organizations. Safeguard any confidential information, vulnerability details, or proprietary data you may come across during your bug hunting activities. Do not disclose such information without proper authorization, even after the vulnerability has been addressed.

Communicate Professionally and Respectfully: Maintain professional and respectful communication with program owners, system administrators, and fellow researchers. Use appropriate language, be patient, and avoid aggressive or confrontational behavior. Professional conduct helps build trust, establishes positive relationships, and promotes collaboration within the bug bounty community.

Continuous Learning and Ethical Development: Stay informed about evolving legal frameworks, ethical standards, and responsible bug hunting practices. Engage in continuous learning and professional development to enhance your knowledge of the legal aspects of bug bounty hunting. Stay up to date with industry best practices, ethical guidelines, and any legal developments that may impact bug hunting activities.

Respecting legal boundaries and guidelines is fundamental to maintaining the integrity and positive impact of bug bounty hunting. By operating within the law, following ethical standards, and adhering to platform and program guidelines, bug hunters can contribute to a safe and responsible bug bounty community, foster trust with program owners, and protect the interests of all stakeholders involved.

9.2 Disclosing Vulnerabilities Responsibly

Disclosing vulnerabilities responsibly is a critical aspect of bug bounty hunting and ethical security research. Responsible disclosure ensures that vulnerabilities are reported and addressed in a manner that prioritizes user safety, protects sensitive information, and allows organizations to implement necessary security measures. In this section, we will explore strategies for responsibly disclosing vulnerabilities.

Understand Responsible Disclosure: Familiarize yourself with the concept of responsible disclosure and the principles it entails. Responsible disclosure emphasizes reporting vulnerabilities directly to the program owner or relevant stakeholders in a timely and coordinated manner, allowing them sufficient time to assess and address the vulnerabilities before public disclosure. Responsible disclosure helps protect users, maintain system integrity, and promote collaboration between bug hunters and organizations.

Follow Program Guidelines: Adhere to the guidelines and disclosure policies set by the bug bounty program or organization. These guidelines may outline specific requirements for reporting vulnerabilities, disclosure timelines, or coordinated disclosure processes. Respecting these guidelines ensures that your disclosure aligns with the program's expectations and facilitates an effective and coordinated response.

Establish Initial Contact: Initiate contact with the program owner or relevant stakeholders to report the vulnerability. Use the designated communication channels or contact information provided by the program. Clearly communicate the nature of the vulnerability, its potential impact, and any necessary technical details. Provide a reliable means of contacting you for further discussion or clarifications.

Allow Time for Remediation: Give the organization a reasonable amount of time to remediate the vulnerability before disclosing it publicly. The specific timeline for remediation may vary depending on the severity and complexity of the vulnerability. Respect the program's disclosure timeline, as agreed upon with the program owner, to allow them to address the issue adequately.

Coordinate Public Disclosure: Work with the program owner to determine an appropriate timeline and method for public disclosure. In some cases, organizations may prefer to disclose the vulnerability themselves after they have applied necessary fixes. Coordinate with them to ensure that the disclosure aligns with their communication strategy and addresses any potential risks.

Anonymous Reporting: If desired or if explicitly allowed by the program, consider anonymous reporting of vulnerabilities. Anonymous reporting can help protect your identity while still allowing the organization to address the vulnerability. Ensure that you follow any specific instructions provided by the program for anonymous reporting.

Provide Clear and Detailed Reports: When reporting vulnerabilities, provide comprehensive and well-documented reports. Clearly describe the vulnerability, including the affected components, steps to reproduce, and potential impact. Include relevant evidence such as screenshots, videos, or proof-of-concept code to support your findings. Clear and detailed reports facilitate the organization's understanding of the vulnerability and help them prioritize remediation efforts.

Respect Confidentiality: Respect any confidentiality or non-disclosure agreements (NDAs) you have entered into with the organization. Safeguard any sensitive information or data you encounter during the bug hunting process. Avoid disclosing vulnerability details or related information outside of authorized channels or without explicit permission from the organization.

Communicate Responsibly: Engage in respectful and professional communication with the organization throughout the disclosure process. Respond promptly to their inquiries, provide clarifications when needed, and address any concerns they may have. Maintain open lines of communication and demonstrate your willingness to assist in the remediation process.

Educate and Advocate Responsible Disclosure: Promote responsible disclosure practices within the bug bounty community and encourage others to follow ethical guidelines. Share your experiences and insights on responsible disclosure through blog posts, presentations, or other educational materials. By advocating responsible disclosure, you contribute to the overall maturity and professionalism of the security research community.

Responsible disclosure demonstrates a commitment to the security of the systems being tested, user privacy, and fostering positive collaboration with organizations. By following responsible disclosure practices, bug bounty hunters play a vital role in helping organizations address vulnerabilities effectively and improve overall security.

9.3 Managing Ethical Dilemmas and Responsible Disclosure

Managing ethical dilemmas and responsible disclosure is an integral part of bug bounty hunting and ethical security research. Bug hunters often encounter complex situations that require careful consideration of ethical principles, legal boundaries, and the potential impact on affected parties. Managing ethical dilemmas effectively and navigating responsible disclosure ensures that vulnerabilities are handled in a manner that prioritizes user safety, respects legal obligations, and promotes responsible behavior within the bug bounty community. In this section, we will explore strategies for managing ethical dilemmas and responsible disclosure.

Understand Ethical Guidelines: Familiarize yourself with established ethical guidelines, such as the Bugcrowd Vulnerability Rating Taxonomy (VRT), the Open Web Application Security Project (OWASP) principles, or other industry standards. These guidelines provide a framework for assessing the severity and impact of vulnerabilities, as well as the appropriate response and disclosure processes.

Consider Potential Impact: Evaluate the potential impact of a vulnerability and the affected parties involved. Assess the severity of the vulnerability, the sensitivity of the data at risk, and the potential harm that could occur if the vulnerability were to be exploited. Consider the balance between responsible disclosure and the potential harm caused by delayed or public disclosure.

Consult with Program Owners or Legal Counsel: Seek guidance from the bug bounty program owners or legal counsel when faced with ethical dilemmas. Engage in open and transparent communication to discuss the situation, potential risks, and the best course of action. Program owners or legal experts can provide insights into legal obligations, disclosure requirements, and the organization's response plans.

Protect User Privacy and Confidentiality: Prioritize user privacy and confidentiality throughout the disclosure process. Handle any personal or sensitive information encountered during bug hunting activities with care and in compliance with applicable data protection regulations. Obtain explicit consent from the program owner before accessing, collecting, or tampering with any personal data.

Balance Public Interest and Disclosure: Assess the public interest in knowing about the vulnerability against the potential risks associated with public disclosure. Consider whether disclosing the vulnerability publicly will lead to immediate exploitation or if providing program owners sufficient time to address the issue is more prudent. Strive to find a balance that protects users, fosters collaboration, and promotes responsible behavior within the bug bounty community.

Coordinated Disclosure: In situations where the vulnerability is critical or widespread, consider coordinated disclosure in consultation with the program owner and other relevant stakeholders. Coordinated disclosure involves sharing vulnerability details with trusted parties, such as the program owner, CERT/CC (Computer Emergency Response Team/Coordination Center), or other appropriate organizations, to ensure that mitigation measures can be implemented simultaneously across affected systems.

Anonymous Reporting: If legal or ethical considerations warrant it, explore the option of anonymous reporting. Anonymous reporting allows you to provide vulnerability details without revealing your identity. Ensure that you follow any specific instructions or procedures provided by the bug bounty program or organization for anonymous reporting.

Engage in Responsible Dialogue: Engage in responsible dialogue with program owners, affected parties, and the bug bounty community when ethical dilemmas arise. Share your concerns, insights, and potential risks associated with the vulnerability. Encourage open and constructive discussions to find the best path forward and ensure that all perspectives are considered.

Documentation and Transparency: Maintain thorough documentation of your ethical decision-making process and disclosure actions. Document the reasoning behind your choices, consultations with program owners or legal counsel, and any agreements or commitments made during the disclosure process. Transparency and clear documentation contribute to accountability and ensure that your actions are defensible.

Continuous Learning and Improvement: Engage in continuous learning and professional development to enhance your understanding of ethical considerations and responsible disclosure practices. Stay informed about legal frameworks, industry guidelines, and evolving ethical standards. Engage in discussions, attend conferences, and participate in relevant training to expand your knowledge and refine your ethical decision-making skills.

Managing ethical dilemmas and responsible disclosure requires a thoughtful and principled approach. By considering the potential impact, consulting with relevant parties, and following established ethical guidelines, bug bounty hunters can navigate these challenges effectively. Responsible disclosure practices promote user safety, protect sensitive information, and contribute to the overall improvement of system security.

Chapter 10: Career Growth in Bug Bounties

Welcome to Chapter 10 of "Bug Bounty Success: How to Become a Top Earner in the Bug Bounty Community." In this chapter, we will explore the exciting possibilities for career growth in the bug bounty community and provide strategies for advancing your bug bounty career to new heights.

Bug bounties offer not only a platform for uncovering vulnerabilities but also a pathway to career development and professional growth. In this chapter, we'll discuss various avenues for advancing your bug bounty career and maximizing your potential as a bug bounty hunter.

We'll begin by exploring the transition to becoming a full-time bug bounty hunter. We'll discuss the considerations and challenges involved in making the leap from a hobbyist to a professional bug bounty hunter. You'll gain insights into financial planning, building a client base, and creating a sustainable bug hunting career.

Freelancing opportunities in the bug bounty community are abundant, and we'll delve into strategies for navigating freelance bug hunting. We'll discuss platforms that connect bug bounty hunters with organizations seeking their expertise, providing you with resources to explore freelance bug hunting opportunities and maximize your earning potential.

Building your personal brand and establishing credibility are crucial for career growth in the bug bounty community. We'll explore strategies for creating a strong online presence, leveraging social media, and showcasing your bug hunting skills through public bug reports, blog posts, and speaking engagements. By establishing a credible personal brand, you'll attract more opportunities and stand out in the bug bounty community.

Professional certifications and qualifications can significantly enhance your bug bounty career. We'll discuss relevant certifications, training programs, and educational resources that can validate your skills and expertise. You'll gain insights into pursuing industry-recognized certifications, attending bug bounty conferences, and engaging in continuous learning to stay ahead in the field.

Mentorship and collaboration are valuable aspects of career growth in bug bounties. We'll explore the benefits of finding mentors and building relationships with experienced bug bounty hunters who can guide you on your journey. Additionally, we'll discuss the power of collaboration, sharing knowledge, and contributing back to the bug bounty community to foster mutual growth and advancement.

Throughout this chapter, we'll emphasize the importance of adaptability and continuous learning for long-term success in bug bounties. The cybersecurity landscape is constantly evolving, and staying updated with new attack techniques, defensive measures, and emerging technologies is crucial for career growth. We'll provide resources and strategies to help you stay at the forefront of the field.

By the end of this chapter, you'll have a roadmap for advancing your bug bounty career. You'll understand the considerations for transitioning to full-time bug hunting, exploring freelance opportunities, and building your personal brand. With the right certifications, mentorship, and continuous learning, you'll be well-equipped to excel in your bug bounty career.

Prepare yourself to unlock new possibilities and accelerate your bug bounty career as we continue our journey towards bug bounty success. In the following chapters, we'll explore bug bounty community engagement, the future of bug bounties, and the importance of continuous learning and adaptability. Let's unleash your full potential as a bug bounty hunter.

10.1 Transitioning to a Full-Time Bug Bounty Hunter

Transitioning to a full-time bug bounty hunter can be an exciting and rewarding career move for those passionate about cybersecurity and ethical hacking. It requires careful planning, continuous skill development, and a strategic approach to maximize earning potential and ensure long-term success. In this section, we will explore strategies and considerations for transitioning to a full-time bug bounty hunter.

Assess Your Skills and Readiness: Evaluate your current skills, knowledge, and experience in bug bounty hunting. Assess your technical proficiency in areas such as web application security, network security, reverse engineering, and mobile application security. Determine if you have the necessary foundation to succeed as a full-time bug bounty hunter or if further skill development is needed.

Build a Strong Reputation: Establishing a strong reputation within the bug bounty community is essential for success. Engage actively in bug bounty platforms, participate in discussions, contribute to open-source projects, and share your knowledge through blog posts or public speaking engagements. Showcase your expertise, ethical conduct, and problem-solving abilities to gain recognition and build trust among program owners.

Develop Diverse Bug Hunting Skills: Expand your bug hunting skills to cover a wide range of vulnerabilities and attack vectors. Continuously learn and stay updated with the latest security trends, emerging technologies, and evolving attack techniques. Enhance your skills in areas such as source code analysis, reverse engineering, cryptographic vulnerabilities, or IoT security to broaden your bug hunting capabilities.

Identify Your Target Market: Identify your target market and focus on bug bounty programs and platforms that align with your interests, expertise, and earning potential. Research industries that are known to have active bug bounty programs, such as technology companies, financial institutions, or government agencies. Assess the competition and the potential for earning higher bounties in your chosen market.

Financial Planning: Before transitioning to full-time bug bounty hunting, carefully consider your financial situation. Bug bounty earnings can be irregular and unpredictable, especially during the initial stages. Ensure you have sufficient savings or alternative sources of income to sustain yourself during periods of low or no bug bounty earnings. Create a budget and plan for necessary expenses, such as tools, training, and professional development.

Networking and Collaboration: Build a strong network within the bug bounty community and collaborate with other bug hunters. Networking can provide valuable opportunities for mentorship, knowledge sharing, and potential collaborations. Engage in bug bounty forums, attend conferences, and participate in bug bounty events to expand your network and stay connected with industry professionals.

Continuous Learning and Skill Development: Commit to continuous learning and skill development to stay ahead in the rapidly evolving cybersecurity landscape. Invest time in researching new attack techniques, attending training programs, obtaining relevant certifications, and participating in Capture the Flag (CTF) competitions. Continuous learning ensures that you remain competitive and adaptable as a bug bounty hunter.

Professionalism and Work Ethics: Maintain a high level of professionalism, ethics, and integrity in your bug hunting activities. Follow responsible disclosure practices, respect program guidelines, and maintain open communication with program owners. Be responsive, reliable, and deliver high-quality vulnerability reports. Professional conduct and strong work ethics contribute to your reputation as a trusted and reliable bug bounty hunter.

Seek Continuous Feedback: Actively seek feedback from program owners and the bug bounty community to improve your skills and performance. Learn from their insights, recommendations, and suggestions for enhancing your bug hunting approach. Implement feedback in a constructive manner to refine your techniques and demonstrate a commitment to continuous improvement.

Diversify Income Sources: Consider diversifying your income sources beyond bug bounties. Explore opportunities for offering security consulting services, providing vulnerability assessments for organizations, or teaching bug hunting courses. Diversifying your income can provide stability during periods of low bug bounty earnings and expand your professional reach.

Transitioning to a full-time bug bounty hunter requires dedication, continuous learning, and a strategic approach. By building a strong reputation, developing diverse bug hunting skills, networking with industry professionals, and maintaining professionalism, you can position yourself for success in this dynamic field. Remember to plan carefully, manage your finances, and embrace the journey of continuous improvement as you embark on your full-time bug bounty hunting career.

10.2 Freelancing Opportunities and Bug Bounty Platforms

Freelancing opportunities in bug bounty hunting have grown significantly, thanks to the increasing demand for cybersecurity expertise and the rise of bug bounty platforms. These platforms connect organizations seeking security testing with skilled bug hunters, providing a platform for earning bounties for responsibly disclosing vulnerabilities. In this section, we will explore popular bug bounty platforms and freelancing opportunities in bug bounty hunting.

Bug Bounty Platforms:

HackerOne: HackerOne is one of the largest bug bounty platforms, hosting a wide range of programs from various organizations. It offers opportunities to work with both small startups and major corporations. HackerOne provides a collaborative environment for bug hunters, allowing them to engage with program owners and the community.

Bugcrowd: Bugcrowd is another well-known bug bounty platform that connects organizations with skilled bug hunters. It offers a diverse range of programs, including private, public, and ongoing programs. Bugcrowd provides bug hunters with resources, support, and a platform to showcase their skills and earn rewards.

Synack: Synack operates a managed crowdsourced security platform that focuses on delivering vulnerability discovery and validation services. It offers flexible opportunities for bug hunters to work on engagements and provides a secure environment for testing critical systems.

Cobalt: Cobalt provides a vulnerability management platform that connects organizations with a global community of ethical hackers. Bug hunters can participate in Cobalt's programs and earn rewards based on the severity and impact of the vulnerabilities discovered.

Open Bug Bounty: Open Bug Bounty is a unique bug bounty platform that focuses on recognizing and rewarding security researchers for responsibly disclosing vulnerabilities in public websites. It allows bug hunters to report vulnerabilities on websites that do not have their own bug bounty programs.

Freelancing Opportunities:

Private Bug Bounties: Some organizations prefer to run private bug bounty programs, exclusively inviting bug hunters to test their systems. Building a reputation and networking within the bug bounty community can lead to invitations for private programs, which often offer higher rewards due to limited competition.

Security Consulting: Freelance bug hunters can offer security consulting services to organizations that require vulnerability assessments, penetration testing, or security advisory services. This provides an opportunity to work directly with clients and earn income beyond bug bounties.

Training and Education: Experienced bug hunters can share their knowledge and skills by offering bug hunting training programs, workshops, or educational courses. This allows them to leverage their expertise to teach and mentor others while generating income.

Public Speaking and Writing: Bug hunters can engage in public speaking engagements, conferences, or webinars to share their experiences and insights. They can also write blog posts, articles, or books to contribute to the cybersecurity community and build their personal brand.

Vulnerability Research: Freelance bug hunters can engage in vulnerability research by exploring emerging technologies, testing popular software, or analyzing novel attack vectors. They can independently discover vulnerabilities and responsibly disclose them to the respective organizations.

When pursuing freelancing opportunities in bug bounty hunting, it is essential to maintain professionalism, follow responsible disclosure practices, and adhere to the guidelines and policies of the platforms and organizations you work with. Building a strong reputation, continuously improving your skills, and nurturing relationships within the bug bounty community can lead to increased freelancing opportunities and a successful bug hunting career.

10.3 Establishing Credibility and Personal Branding

Establishing credibility and personal branding is crucial for bug bounty hunters to stand out in a competitive field, attract lucrative opportunities, and build trust with program owners and the bug bounty community. By effectively showcasing their skills, professionalism, and expertise, bug bounty hunters can establish a strong reputation and elevate their career. In this section, we will explore strategies for establishing credibility and personal branding in the bug bounty community.

Develop Technical Expertise: Continuously improve your technical skills and knowledge in areas relevant to bug bounty hunting. Stay updated with the latest security trends, vulnerabilities, and hacking techniques. Specialize in specific domains, such as web application security, mobile application security, or network security, to showcase your expertise in those areas.

Actively Engage in Bug Bounty Platforms: Participate actively in bug bounty platforms such as HackerOne, Bugcrowd, or others. Engage with program owners, participate in bug hunting challenges, and provide valuable insights in discussions. Consistently report high-quality vulnerabilities and maintain a positive track record on these platforms.

Publish Research and Write-ups: Share your bug hunting experiences, research findings, and insights through blog posts, whitepapers, or technical write-ups. Document your methodology, successful discoveries, and lessons learned. Publishing your work not only helps establish credibility but also contributes to the broader security community.

Contribute to Open-Source Projects: Contribute to open-source projects related to cybersecurity, bug hunting tools, or vulnerability research. Actively engage in discussions, submit bug reports, or contribute code enhancements. Contributing to open-source projects demonstrates your expertise and commitment to the community.

Speak at Conferences and Events: Apply to speak at cybersecurity conferences, webinars, or local meetups to share your knowledge and experiences. Presenting at industry events allows you to showcase your expertise, build connections, and gain visibility among industry professionals and potential clients.

Engage in Responsible Disclosure Advocacy: Actively promote responsible disclosure practices within the bug bounty community. Share your insights and experiences related to responsible disclosure, ethical hacking, and vulnerability management. Advocate for collaborative approaches that prioritize user safety and facilitate effective vulnerability remediation.

Network with Peers and Program Owners: Actively network with fellow bug hunters, program owners, and industry professionals. Engage in bug bounty forums, join relevant communities, and attend security conferences or meetups. Building relationships within the bug bounty community helps establish credibility, opens doors to collaborative opportunities, and enables knowledge sharing.

Maintain Professionalism and Ethical Conduct: Conduct yourself with professionalism, integrity, and strong ethics in all your bug hunting activities. Follow responsible disclosure practices, respect program guidelines, and maintain open and respectful communication with program owners. Professionalism and ethical conduct contribute to building trust and a positive reputation.

Seek Recommendations and Testimonials: Request recommendations or testimonials from program owners or fellow bug hunters with whom you have collaborated. These endorsements provide social proof of your skills, work ethic, and professionalism, and can bolster your credibility when seeking new opportunities.

Continuously Learn and Improve: Stay committed to continuous learning and improvement. Attend training programs, obtain relevant certifications, and participate in Capture the Flag (CTF) competitions to enhance your skills. Embrace feedback and actively seek opportunities for growth and development.

Establishing credibility and personal branding requires consistent effort, dedication, and a commitment to excellence. By showcasing technical expertise, actively engaging in the bug bounty community, sharing knowledge, and maintaining professionalism, bug bounty hunters can build a strong personal brand that attracts rewarding opportunities and fosters long-term success in the field.

Chapter 11: Bug Bounty Community Engagement

Welcome to Chapter 11 of "Bug Bounty Success: How to Become a Top Earner in the Bug Bounty Community." In this chapter, we will delve into the importance of community engagement in the bug bounty world and provide strategies for actively participating and contributing to the bug bounty community.

The bug bounty community is a vibrant and collaborative space where researchers come together to share knowledge, learn from one another, and collectively enhance the cybersecurity landscape. In this chapter, we'll explore the benefits of community engagement and guide you on how to actively participate in and contribute to the bug bounty community.

We'll begin by discussing the value of networking within the bug bounty community. Building connections and relationships with fellow researchers can provide numerous benefits, including knowledge sharing, collaboration on bug reports, and opportunities for mentorship. We'll explore strategies for networking, such as attending bug bounty conferences, joining online communities, and engaging in bug bounty platforms' discussion forums.

Sharing knowledge and experiences is a vital aspect of community engagement. We'll discuss the power of contributing back to the community through blog posts, tutorials, and public bug reports. By sharing your insights and discoveries, you not only help others learn and grow but also establish yourself as a reputable and respected member of the bug bounty community.

Mentorship plays a significant role in the bug bounty community. We'll explore the benefits of finding mentors and mentors who can provide guidance, advice, and support on your bug bounty journey. We'll discuss strategies for seeking out mentors, building relationships, and fostering a mentorship dynamic that can contribute to your growth as a bug bounty hunter.

Contributing to open-source projects and bug bounty tools is another valuable way to engage with the community. We'll explore the benefits of contributing code, documentation, or bug reports to open-source projects that support the bug bounty ecosystem. By actively participating in these projects, you'll not only enhance your skills but also contribute to the advancement of the bug bounty community as a whole.

Additionally, we'll discuss the importance of ethical collaboration and responsible disclosure within the bug bounty community. Collaboration can lead to improved bug hunting techniques, shared insights, and a collective effort towards a safer digital landscape. We'll explore ways to collaborate responsibly, share information securely, and promote a positive and ethical bug bounty community.

Throughout this chapter, we'll emphasize the significance of giving back and actively participating in the bug bounty community. By engaging with fellow researchers, sharing knowledge, seeking mentorship, and collaborating ethically, you'll become an integral part of the bug bounty ecosystem and contribute to its growth and development.

By the end of this chapter, you'll understand the value of community engagement in the bug bounty world. You'll have strategies for networking, sharing knowledge, seeking mentorship, and contributing to open-source projects. Through active participation in the bug bounty community, you'll not only enhance your bug hunting skills but also foster meaningful connections and contribute to the collective knowledge and growth of the community.

Prepare yourself to actively engage with the bug bounty community as we continue our journey towards bug bounty success. In the following chapters, we'll explore the future of bug bounties, continuous learning, and adaptability in the rapidly evolving cybersecurity landscape. Let's strengthen our bonds within the bug bounty community and make a positive impact together.

11.1 Participating in Bug Bounty Events and Conferences

Participating in bug bounty events and conferences is a valuable opportunity for bug bounty hunters to enhance their skills, expand their professional network, and stay updated with the latest trends in the industry. These events provide a platform for learning from experts, sharing experiences, and building connections with program owners, fellow bug hunters, and cybersecurity professionals. In this section, we will explore the benefits and strategies for participating in bug bounty events and conferences.

Benefits of Participating in Bug Bounty Events and Conferences:

Learning Opportunities: Bug bounty events and conferences feature presentations, workshops, and training sessions delivered by industry experts. Attendees can learn about the latest hacking techniques, emerging vulnerabilities, and defensive strategies. These events offer a unique opportunity to gain insights from experienced professionals and expand your knowledge base.

Networking: Bug bounty events bring together a diverse group of professionals, including bug hunters, program owners, security researchers, and cybersecurity enthusiasts. Engaging in conversations, networking sessions, and social events allows you to build connections, exchange ideas, and establish relationships with peers and industry leaders. Networking can lead to collaborative opportunities, mentorship, or even job offers.

Showcasing Your Expertise: Bug bounty events often provide platforms for bug hunters to present their research findings, share their experiences, or participate in Capture the Flag (CTF) competitions. Presenting your work allows you to showcase your technical skills, problem-solving abilities, and expertise. It helps establish your credibility and enhances your professional reputation within the bug bounty community.

Discovering New Bug Bounty Programs: Bug bounty events provide an opportunity to learn about new bug bounty programs and initiatives. Program owners often participate in these events to connect with bug hunters and promote their programs. By attending these events, you can discover new opportunities for bug hunting engagements and gain early access to exclusive programs.

Staying Updated with Industry Trends: Bug bounty events and conferences are excellent platforms to stay updated with the latest industry trends, best practices, and regulatory changes. Keynote speeches, panel discussions, and interactive sessions provide insights into emerging threats, cutting-edge security technologies, and policy developments. Staying informed enables you to adapt your bug hunting strategies and remain relevant in the ever-evolving field of cybersecurity.

Strategies for Participating in Bug Bounty Events and Conferences:

Research Event Opportunities: Stay informed about upcoming bug bounty events, conferences, or workshops through professional networks, social media, or industry websites. Research the event agenda, speakers, and attendees to ensure alignment with your interests and goals. Choose events that provide relevant content, networking opportunities, and participation options suitable for your needs.

Prepare Your Elevator Pitch: Craft a concise and compelling elevator pitch that introduces yourself, highlights your bug hunting expertise, and emphasizes your unique skills or research interests. This helps in initiating conversations with fellow participants, program owners, or potential collaborators. Practice your pitch beforehand to ensure clarity and confidence.

Engage Actively: Actively participate in sessions, workshops, and networking activities during the event. Ask questions, share your experiences, and engage in discussions. Actively contributing to the conversations demonstrates your enthusiasm, knowledge, and willingness to learn from others.

Attend Relevant Sessions: Plan your schedule to attend sessions, workshops, or presentations that align with your areas of interest or areas where you aim to enhance your skills. Prioritize sessions delivered by experts in your field of specialization or those covering emerging technologies and vulnerabilities.

Network Effectively: Actively engage in networking opportunities such as coffee breaks, networking sessions, or social events. Approach fellow attendees, introduce yourself, and initiate conversations. Be genuinely interested in their work and experiences. Exchange contact information and follow up with meaningful interactions after the event.

Present Your Research: If you have conducted notable bug hunting research or made significant discoveries, consider submitting a presentation or workshop proposal. Presenting your research allows you to share your findings, gain feedback from experts, and establish yourself as an authority in your field. Follow the event's guidelines and submission deadlines when preparing your presentation or workshop proposal.

Participate in Capture the Flag (CTF) Competitions: Take part in bug bounty-related Capture the Flag competitions organized as part of the event. CTF competitions provide hands-on experience, allow you to test your skills, and compete with fellow bug hunters. They also offer opportunities to learn from other participants and showcase your problem-solving abilities.

Follow up and Stay Connected: After the event, follow up with the people you connected with, such as fellow attendees, program owners, or potential collaborators. Send personalized follow-up emails, connect on professional networking platforms, and nurture the relationships you formed during the event. Staying connected allows for ongoing collaboration and knowledge sharing.

Participating in bug bounty events and conferences provides a unique opportunity to enhance your bug hunting skills, expand your network, and establish your presence within the bug bounty community. By preparing effectively, engaging actively, and leveraging the learning and networking opportunities available, you can maximize the benefits of these events and further your bug bounty hunting career.

11.2 Sharing Knowledge and Contributing to the Community

Sharing knowledge and contributing to the bug bounty community is not only a way to give back but also a means to enhance your own skills, build a strong professional network, and establish yourself as a trusted and respected bug bounty hunter. By actively sharing your experiences, insights, and expertise, you contribute to the growth and development of the community as a whole. In this section, we will explore strategies for sharing knowledge and contributing to the bug bounty community.

Blogging and Technical Writing: Start a blog or contribute guest posts to established cybersecurity blogs. Share your bug hunting experiences, successful findings, methodologies, and insights on emerging vulnerabilities or attack techniques. Write in a clear and concise manner, focusing on practical takeaways and actionable advice. Consider creating tutorials or walkthroughs to help others understand complex concepts.

Open-Source Contributions: Contribute to open-source projects related to bug hunting tools, vulnerability scanners, or security frameworks. Submit code enhancements, bug reports, or documentation updates. Actively engage with the project community, provide feedback, and share your expertise to help improve the tools or frameworks used by bug hunters.

Mentorship and Collaboration: Offer mentorship to aspiring bug hunters or those looking to enhance their skills. Share your experiences, provide guidance on methodologies and techniques, and assist with problem-solving. Collaborate with other bug hunters on projects or bug bounty programs, leveraging the collective knowledge and skills of the community.

Presentations and Workshops: Participate in bug bounty conferences, meetups, or webinars as a speaker or workshop facilitator. Share your bug hunting experiences, present your research findings, and provide insights on effective bug hunting techniques. Engage with the audience, encourage questions, and foster a collaborative learning environment.

Online Forums and Communities: Participate actively in bug bounty forums, subreddits, and online communities. Share your expertise, answer questions, and engage in discussions related to bug hunting, vulnerability analysis, or responsible disclosure. Be respectful, constructive, and willing to learn from others.

Capture the Flag (CTF) Competitions: Participate in bug bounty-related Capture the Flag (CTF) competitions. These events allow you to test your skills, solve real-world scenarios, and collaborate with other bug hunters. Share your CTF experiences, strategies, and challenges faced, fostering a culture of learning and growth within the community.

Code Contributions and Research Tools: Develop and share bug hunting tools, scripts, or utilities that can assist other bug hunters in their work. Contribute to public repositories or create your own GitHub repository for others to access and benefit from your work. Encourage feedback, collaboration, and improvements from the community.

Responsible Disclosure Advocacy: Advocate for responsible disclosure practices within the bug bounty community and beyond. Educate others about the importance of responsible disclosure, the impact of vulnerabilities, and the value of collaboration between bug hunters and program owners. Engage in discussions, write articles, or participate in podcasts to raise awareness about responsible disclosure.

Bug Bounty Program Feedback: Provide constructive feedback to bug bounty platforms and program owners to help improve their processes, guidelines, and platform features. Share your experiences as a bug hunter and suggest enhancements that can make bug hunting programs more effective, efficient, and rewarding.

Continuous Learning and Sharing: Commit to continuous learning and stay updated with the latest trends, vulnerabilities, and security techniques. Share your discoveries, research papers, or articles that contribute to the overall knowledge base of the bug bounty community. Actively engage with others who are sharing their knowledge to create a collaborative and supportive environment.

By sharing knowledge, collaborating with others, and actively contributing to the bug bounty community, you not only help others grow but also establish yourself as a valuable resource within the community. The sharing of knowledge fosters innovation, encourages responsible practices, and elevates the entire bug bounty ecosystem.

11.3 Mentorship and Collaboration Opportunities

Engaging in mentorship and collaboration opportunities within the bug bounty community is a valuable way to contribute to the growth and development of aspiring bug hunters, foster a sense of community, and enhance your own skills through shared knowledge and experiences. Mentorship allows you to guide others on their bug bounty journey, while collaboration enables you to leverage the collective expertise of the community. In this section, we will explore strategies for mentorship and collaboration in the bug bounty community.

Mentorship Opportunities:

Offer Guidance and Support: Share your experiences, insights, and lessons learned with aspiring bug hunters. Provide guidance on bug hunting methodologies, tools, and techniques. Help mentees understand the bug bounty ecosystem, navigate platforms, and engage with program owners. Offer encouragement and support throughout their bug bounty journey.

Foster a Learning Environment: Create a safe and inclusive environment for learning and growth. Encourage mentees to ask questions, explore new vulnerabilities, and share their findings. Provide constructive feedback and guidance on vulnerability reports, methodologies, and approaches. Foster a collaborative atmosphere where mentees feel comfortable seeking advice and sharing their progress.

Set Realistic Goals: Help mentees set realistic and achievable goals based on their skill level and interests. Break down their objectives into smaller milestones and guide them in developing a roadmap to achieve those goals. Encourage them to pursue continuous learning and improvement.

Review and Provide Feedback: Review vulnerability reports, methodologies, and research findings shared by your mentees. Provide constructive feedback on their approach, documentation, and overall quality. Help them understand areas for improvement and offer suggestions for enhancing their bug hunting skills.

Share Resources: Share relevant resources, such as tutorials, articles, research papers, or recommended reading materials, to support the learning process. Provide guidance on useful bug hunting tools, frameworks, and platforms. Point mentees to reputable sources of information and educational platforms to enhance their knowledge.

Collaboration Opportunities:

Collaborative Bug Hunting: Collaborate with other bug hunters on specific projects or bug bounty programs. Pool your collective knowledge, skills, and experiences to tackle complex targets or vulnerabilities. Share insights, divide research tasks, and collaborate on vulnerability analysis and exploitation.

Capture the Flag (CTF) Competitions: Participate in Capture the Flag (CTF) competitions as a team. Collaborate with fellow bug hunters to solve challenges, exploit vulnerabilities, and earn points. Collaborative CTF competitions provide an opportunity to learn from others, share tactics, and work together to achieve common goals.

Research Projects: Collaborate on research projects focused on exploring new attack vectors, testing emerging technologies, or analyzing specific vulnerabilities. Share the workload, research findings, and insights. Collaborative research projects allow for a deeper understanding of complex security issues and promote knowledge sharing within the community.

Bug Bounty Program Collaboration: Collaborate with other bug hunters on specific bug bounty programs. Share insights, coordinate testing efforts, and avoid duplicating research. Collaborative efforts can help discover vulnerabilities more efficiently and enhance the overall quality of the bug reports submitted to program owners.

Knowledge Exchange: Actively engage in discussions and knowledge-sharing platforms within the bug bounty community. Share your experiences, insights, and research findings. Contribute to forums, online communities, or chat groups dedicated to bug hunting. Participate in bug bounty-related conferences, meetups, or webinars where you can network and collaborate with like-minded professionals.

Benefits of Mentorship and Collaboration:

Personal Growth: Mentoring and collaborating with others allows you to reinforce and deepen your own knowledge and skills. Explaining concepts and providing guidance to mentees helps solidify your own understanding of bug hunting techniques and methodologies. Collaborative efforts expose you to diverse perspectives and strategies, broadening your horizons and expanding your problem-solving abilities.

Building a Supportive Community: By engaging in mentorship and collaboration, you contribute to the development of a supportive bug bounty community. Encouraging and assisting others fosters a positive and inclusive environment where everyone can learn, grow, and achieve their potential. This sense of community strengthens the bug bounty ecosystem as a whole.

Networking and Professional Opportunities: Mentorship and collaboration often lead to valuable networking opportunities. Mentees may go on to become successful bug hunters, program owners, or industry professionals, and they may provide opportunities for collaboration or recommend you for future projects. Building strong relationships within the bug bounty community can open doors to new professional opportunities and collaborations.

Giving Back and Paying It Forward: Mentorship and collaboration allow you to give back to the community by sharing your knowledge and experiences. Helping others on their bug bounty journey can have a lasting impact on their professional growth and success. By paying it forward, you contribute to the development and sustainability of the bug bounty community.

By engaging in mentorship and collaboration, you contribute to the growth and development of the bug bounty community while enhancing your own skills and professional network. Sharing knowledge, providing guidance, and collaborating with others fosters a supportive environment where bug hunters can learn, thrive, and make a positive impact on the security landscape.

Chapter 12: The Future of Bug Bounties

Welcome to Chapter 12, the final chapter of "Bug Bounty Success: How to Become a Top Earner in the Bug Bounty Community." In this chapter, we will explore the future of bug bounties and discuss emerging trends and developments that will shape the bug bounty landscape.

Bug bounties have come a long way, revolutionizing the cybersecurity industry and providing opportunities for talented individuals to contribute to digital security. As we look ahead, it's crucial to understand the evolving nature of bug bounties and adapt to the changes that lie ahead.

We'll begin by exploring the increasing adoption of bug bounties by organizations. As more businesses recognize the value of crowd-sourced security testing, we can expect to see a continued growth in the number of bug bounty programs across various industries. This expansion presents new opportunities for bug bounty hunters to engage with a broader range of organizations and uncover vulnerabilities in previously unexplored areas.

Automation and artificial intelligence (AI) will play a significant role in the future of bug bounties. We'll discuss the integration of automated vulnerability scanners, machine learning algorithms, and AI-powered analysis tools into bug bounty platforms. These advancements will help streamline the bug hunting process, improve vulnerability detection, and enhance the efficiency of bug bounty programs.

Bug bounty programs will increasingly focus on emerging technologies and sectors. As technology evolves, new attack surfaces and vulnerabilities emerge. We'll explore the potential impact of bug bounties in areas such as Internet of Things (IoT), cloud computing, blockchain, and artificial intelligence. By staying ahead of these emerging trends, bug bounty hunters can position themselves as experts in cutting-edge technologies.

Collaboration and collective defense will become more prevalent in the bug bounty community. Bug bounty platforms and organizations will foster greater collaboration among researchers, encouraging the sharing of insights, techniques, and vulnerabilities. Bug bounty hunters will increasingly work together on complex bug chains and systemic vulnerabilities, leading to more impactful bug reports and improved security for organizations.

We'll also discuss the growing focus on diversity and inclusion within the bug bounty community. Recognizing the importance of diverse perspectives, bug bounty programs and platforms will work towards creating an inclusive environment that welcomes individuals from all backgrounds. This inclusivity will help foster innovation, broaden the pool of bug hunters, and strengthen the community as a whole.

Lastly, we'll explore the increasing professionalization of bug bounty hunting. As bug bounties gain mainstream recognition, we can expect to see more standardized qualifications, certifications, and professional associations for bug bounty hunters. These developments will provide bug hunters with opportunities for career growth, recognition, and enhanced professional development.

By understanding the future trends and developments in bug bounties, you can position yourself to adapt and thrive in this evolving landscape. Embracing automation, staying at the forefront of emerging technologies, fostering collaboration, promoting diversity, and embracing professionalization will contribute to your long-term success as a bug bounty hunter.

As we conclude this book, I want to commend you for embarking on this bug bounty journey. The world of bug bounties offers endless opportunities for learning, growth, and making a positive impact on digital security. By applying the knowledge and strategies shared in this book, you are well on your way to becoming a top earner in the bug bounty community.

Remember, bug bounty success requires dedication, continuous learning, ethical conduct, and active community engagement. Stay curious, adapt to the changing landscape, and always strive for excellence in your bug hunting endeavors.

12.1 Emerging Trends and Technologies

Staying informed about emerging trends and technologies is crucial for bug bounty hunters to remain relevant, adapt their skills, and effectively identify vulnerabilities in new systems and platforms. The ever-evolving technology landscape introduces new attack vectors, security challenges, and opportunities for bug hunters. In this section, we will explore some of the emerging trends and technologies that bug bounty hunters should be aware of.

Internet of Things (IoT): The proliferation of IoT devices presents new challenges and opportunities for bug hunters. IoT devices, such as smart home appliances, wearables, and industrial control systems, often have unique attack surfaces and vulnerabilities. Understanding the architecture, protocols, and security measures of IoT ecosystems is essential for identifying vulnerabilities in these emerging technologies.

Cloud Computing: Cloud platforms and services have become a fundamental component of modern infrastructure. Bug hunters need to familiarize themselves with cloud technologies, such as Amazon Web Services (AWS), Microsoft Azure, and Google Cloud Platform (GCP). Understanding cloud-specific security considerations, misconfigurations, and vulnerabilities allows bug hunters to identify potential weaknesses and secure cloud-based systems effectively.

Mobile Application Security: Mobile applications continue to dominate the digital landscape. Bug hunters should stay updated with the latest mobile app development frameworks, security features, and emerging mobile threats. Knowledge of mobile platforms (iOS and Android), reverse engineering techniques, and secure coding practices is crucial for identifying vulnerabilities in mobile apps.

Web Application Technologies: Web applications remain a prime target for attackers. Bug hunters must keep up with advancements in web application frameworks, programming languages, and security measures. Technologies such as JavaScript frameworks (React, Angular, Vue.js), GraphQL, Single-Page Applications (SPAs), and serverless architectures are evolving rapidly, introducing new attack vectors and security considerations.

Artificial Intelligence (AI) and Machine Learning (ML): The integration of AI and ML into various applications and systems brings new security challenges. Understanding how AI algorithms work, potential vulnerabilities in ML models, and the security implications of AI-powered systems is essential for bug hunters. AI-based security tools, adversarial attacks, and privacy concerns related to AI should also be on their radar.

Blockchain and Cryptocurrencies: As blockchain technology and cryptocurrencies gain traction, bug hunters should familiarize themselves with the security aspects of decentralized systems. Understanding smart contracts, blockchain consensus mechanisms, and vulnerabilities specific to blockchain applications allows bug hunters to identify potential weaknesses in these systems.

Edge Computing: Edge computing involves processing data closer to the source, reducing latency and enhancing efficiency. Bug hunters should be aware of the security implications of edge computing architectures, edge devices, and communication protocols. Identifying vulnerabilities in edge computing systems ensures the security of data processing at the network edge.

Biometric Security: Biometric authentication methods, such as fingerprint scanning and facial recognition, are increasingly used in various applications. Bug hunters need to understand the security mechanisms and potential vulnerabilities associated with biometric systems. Evaluating the resilience of biometric authentication against spoofing attacks or other vulnerabilities is crucial.

Automotive and Transportation Security: The rise of connected and autonomous vehicles introduces unique security challenges. Bug hunters should stay informed about automotive cybersecurity trends, including vulnerabilities in vehicle systems, communication protocols, and in-vehicle software. Understanding the security of automotive interfaces, such as Controller Area Network (CAN) buses, is essential for identifying potential risks.

Privacy and Data Protection: Privacy concerns and data protection regulations continue to be at the forefront of cybersecurity discussions. Bug hunters should stay updated with evolving privacy laws, such as the General Data Protection Regulation (GDPR) and the California Consumer Privacy Act (CCPA). Understanding privacy implications, data handling practices, and potential vulnerabilities related to personal data protection is crucial.

It's important for bug bounty hunters to proactively research and study these emerging trends and technologies. Engaging in hands-on experimentation, participating in related bug bounty programs, attending conferences, and collaborating with other professionals in the field are effective strategies to stay ahead of the curve. Adapting their bug hunting methodologies and skill sets to address emerging trends ensures that bug hunters remain effective and continue to contribute to the security of evolving systems and technologies.

12.2 Predictions for the Bug Bounty Landscape

Predicting the future of the bug bounty landscape is a challenging task, as it is influenced by various factors, including technological advancements, evolving threat landscapes, and industry trends. However, based on current observations and patterns, we can make some predictions regarding the bug bounty landscape:

Increased Adoption and Growth: Bug bounty programs will continue to gain traction as organizations recognize the value of crowdsourced security testing. More companies, including those outside the technology sector, will launch bug bounty programs to proactively identify vulnerabilities in their systems and enhance their security posture.

Expansion into New Industries: Bug bounty programs will expand beyond traditional technology companies, reaching industries such as finance, healthcare, automotive, and government sectors. As these sectors become more digitally focused, they will embrace bug bounty programs as an effective means of identifying security vulnerabilities.

Emphasis on IoT Security: With the proliferation of Internet of Things (IoT) devices, bug bounty programs will increasingly focus on identifying vulnerabilities in IoT ecosystems. The interconnected nature of these devices introduces unique security challenges, making IoT security a critical area of concern for organizations.

Collaboration between Bug Hunters and AI Systems: Bug hunters will leverage artificial intelligence (AI) and machine learning (ML) technologies to enhance their bug hunting capabilities. AI-powered tools will help automate vulnerability scanning, triage bug reports, and identify patterns in security vulnerabilities, enabling bug hunters to work more efficiently.

Integration of Bug Bounty Platforms and Security Testing Tools: Bug bounty platforms will integrate with security testing tools, enabling bug hunters to seamlessly perform security assessments, vulnerability scanning, and penetration testing. This integration will streamline the bug hunting process and provide a more comprehensive testing environment.

Enhanced Recognition and Rewards: Organizations will offer increased recognition and higher monetary rewards for bug hunters who consistently demonstrate exceptional skills and discover critical vulnerabilities. Bug bounty programs will introduce additional incentives, such as leaderboard rankings, public acknowledgment, and exclusive invitations to private programs.

Continuous Learning and Skill Development: Bug bounty hunters will prioritize continuous learning and skill development to keep pace with evolving technologies and attack vectors. They will engage in specialized training programs, obtain relevant certifications, and participate in Capture the Flag (CTF) competitions to enhance their skills and stay competitive.

Global Bug Bounty Collaboration: Bug bounty hunters from different regions will collaborate more closely, sharing insights, strategies, and experiences. Global bug bounty platforms and communities will facilitate this collaboration, fostering a sense of global cooperation and knowledge sharing among bug hunters.

Enhanced Program Scope and Complexity: Bug bounty programs will expand their scope beyond traditional web and mobile applications, targeting emerging technologies such as blockchain, AI systems, and edge computing. The complexity of bug bounty programs will increase, requiring bug hunters to possess a diverse skill set and deep understanding of these technologies.

Regulatory Influence: The bug bounty landscape will be influenced by evolving cybersecurity regulations and privacy laws. Organizations will integrate bug bounty programs into their compliance strategies to demonstrate a commitment to security and compliance with data protection regulations.

It's important to note that these predictions are speculative, and the bug bounty landscape may evolve in ways that are currently unforeseen. Nevertheless, bug bounty hunters can prepare themselves by staying updated with emerging technologies, continuously improving their skills, and actively participating in the bug bounty community to adapt to the changing landscape.

12.3 Continuous Learning and Adaptability for Long-Term Success

Continuous learning and adaptability are key factors for long-term success in the bug bounty community. As technology evolves and new vulnerabilities emerge, bug bounty hunters must stay up-to-date with the latest trends, techniques, and tools to effectively identify and exploit vulnerabilities. In this section, we will explore the importance of continuous learning and adaptability and provide strategies for bug bounty hunters to embrace them.

Stay Informed: Stay abreast of the latest developments in cybersecurity, including emerging technologies, attack vectors, and defense mechanisms. Follow reputable sources such as security blogs, research papers, industry reports, and conferences. Engage in online communities, forums, and social media groups dedicated to bug hunting to exchange knowledge and stay informed about the latest trends.

Professional Development: Invest in your professional development by attending training programs, workshops, and webinars that focus on bug hunting, penetration testing, secure coding, and related topics. Obtain relevant certifications, such as Certified Ethical Hacker (CEH), Offensive Security Certified Professional (OSCP), or Certified Web Application Hacker (CWAH), to validate your skills and enhance your credibility.

Participate in Capture the Flag (CTF) Competitions: Engage in CTF competitions, both online and offline, to enhance your problem-solving abilities, improve your technical skills, and expose yourself to real-world scenarios. CTF challenges offer practical hands-on experience and provide opportunities to learn from peers and experts.

Experiment and Research: Set up your own testing environment to experiment with different tools, frameworks, and technologies. Conduct independent research to identify new attack vectors, analyze emerging vulnerabilities, or explore unconventional bug hunting techniques. Document your findings and share them with the bug bounty community.

Collaborate with Peers: Collaborate with other bug bounty hunters, researchers, and professionals in the cybersecurity field. Engage in joint projects, participate in bug bounty programs as a team, or share insights and experiences. Collaborating with peers not only expands your knowledge base but also exposes you to different perspectives and approaches.

Learn from Bug Reports: Study and analyze bug reports submitted by other bug bounty hunters. Understand the methodologies, techniques, and creative approaches used by successful bug hunters. Learn from their experiences and apply their insights to your own bug hunting endeavors.

Embrace Feedback: Be open to feedback from program owners, peers, and the bug bounty community. Actively seek feedback on your vulnerability reports, methodologies, and techniques. Embracing feedback helps you identify areas for improvement, refine your skills, and grow as a bug bounty hunter.

Adapt to New Technologies: Stay ahead of the curve by familiarizing yourself with emerging technologies, such as IoT, blockchain, cloud computing, and AI. Understand their security implications, attack surfaces, and vulnerabilities. Adapt your bug hunting strategies to accommodate these technologies and identify potential weaknesses.

Learn from Failure: Bug hunting involves trial and error. Embrace failures as learning opportunities. Analyze unsuccessful attempts, understand the reasons for failure, and extract valuable lessons. Persistence, resilience, and the ability to learn from failures are essential for long-term success in the bug bounty community.

Contribute to the Community: Share your knowledge, experiences, and insights with the bug bounty community. Write blog posts, publish research papers, deliver presentations, and actively participate in discussions. Contributing to the community not only helps others but also enhances your own understanding of the subject matter.

Continuous learning and adaptability are integral to staying relevant and effective in the bug bounty landscape. By embracing these principles and actively seeking new knowledge and experiences, bug bounty hunters can position themselves for long-term success, contribute to the security community, and make a meaningful impact in the fight against cybersecurity threats.

Congratulations on completing **"Bug Bounty Success: How to Become a Top Earner in the Bug Bounty Community"**! Throughout this book, we've explored the exciting world of bug bounties and uncovered the strategies and insights needed to excel in this dynamic field.

From the early chapters, where we laid the groundwork and introduced you to bug bounty programs, to the practical techniques and tools shared in subsequent chapters, you've gained a comprehensive understanding of the skills necessary for bug hunting success.

We've delved into the mindset required for effective bug hunting, emphasizing the importance of perseverance, continuous learning, and embracing a hacker's mentality. You've learned how to think outside the box, creatively identify vulnerabilities, and validate your findings.

Maximizing your bug bounty earnings has been a focal point, and you've discovered the strategies for selecting high-value targets, exploiting impactful vulnerabilities, and reporting your findings in a clear and effective manner. By prioritizing and honing your bug hunting skills, you're now well-equipped to maximize your rewards.

Throughout this journey, we've explored bug bounty platforms, emphasizing their features, rewards, and the community that surrounds them. You've learned how to leverage automation and collaborate with other researchers, fostering connections that enhance your bug hunting capabilities.

Maintaining professional relationships with organizations has been another key aspect. By establishing effective communication channels, responsibly disclosing vulnerabilities, and building long-term partnerships, you're well-positioned to navigate the bug bounty landscape with integrity and professionalism.

Real-life case studies have provided valuable insights, showcasing successful bug reports and the impact they had on the organizations involved. By analyzing these cases, you've gained valuable knowledge and inspiration, fueling your bug hunting endeavors.

Ethics and responsible disclosure have been recurring themes throughout this book. You've learned to respect legal boundaries, navigate ethical dilemmas, and contribute to a safer digital environment. By upholding these principles, you've positioned yourself as a trusted and respected member of the bug bounty community.

Looking ahead, we explored the career growth potential within bug bounties, discussing the possibilities of transitioning to full-time bug hunting, freelancing, and establishing your personal brand. You now have the tools and strategies to propel your bug bounty career to new heights.

Finally, we emphasized the importance of community engagement. By participating in bug bounty events, sharing knowledge, and collaborating with others, you've become an active contributor to the ever-growing bug bounty community, fostering mutual growth and learning.

As you close this book, remember that bug bounty success is an ongoing journey. The cybersecurity landscape is constantly evolving, presenting new challenges and opportunities. Stay curious, continue learning, and adapt to emerging trends and technologies.

Thank you for joining me on this bug bounty adventure. I hope that the knowledge, insights, and strategies shared in this book have inspired you and equipped you for success in the bug bounty community. Now, it's time to embark on your own bug hunting endeavors, making a positive impact while becoming a top earner in the bug bounty world.

Happy bug hunting!